I'm Faithful, But I'm Not Religious

Chuck & Sharon,

You have always made me feel like a part of the family. I thank you.

Peace

Ed Sinclair

2007

I'm Faithful, But I'm Not Religious

◆

Musings of a Cynical Mystic

Edward A. Sinclair

iUniverse, Inc.
New York Lincoln Shanghai

I'm Faithful, But I'm Not Religious
Musings of a Cynical Mystic

Copyright © 2006 by Edward A. Sinclair

iUniverse books may be ordered through booksellers or by contacting:

iUniverse
2021 Pine Lake Road, Suite 100
Lincoln, NE 68512
www.iuniverse.com
1-800-Authors (1-800-288-4677)

ISBN-13: 978-0-595-40581-7 (pbk)
ISBN-13: 978-0-595-84947-5 (ebk)
ISBN-10: 0-595-40581-9 (pbk)
ISBN-10: 0-595-84947-4 (ebk)

Printed in the United States of America

I dedicate this work to my sister, Annie. While still a baby, death claimed her. My first mystical experience was when she spoke to me five years after her death. If only I'd known then what I know now.

Contents

GETTING HEALED UP

SOME LESSONS LEARNED

MAY I ASK WHO IS CALLING?

WALKING THE WALK

UP TO THE CHALLENGE?

FINAL THOUGHT

Foreword

Many people over the years have encouraged me to write a book. My response has always been, "What on earth for?" I started composing music and lyrics when I was ten years old; I still compose music and lyrics. Short, succinct, four-line stanzas that rhyme most times (but sometimes don't) have been my literary genre of choice. I write like I go to the store; I go in, I do what needs to be done as quickly as possible, and I go home. The idea of writing prose has always felt foreign and burdensome to me. Nonetheless, the requests to write down some of my reflections have continued.

Not long ago, a thought occurred to me. If I were to commit myself to writing no more than a page or two at one time, the task would not be all that daunting. So, that's what I set out to do. As a form of self-discipline, I used, as my basis, the daily scripture guide published by the American Bible Society. The guide provided the stimulation, I provided the opinions.

Acknowledgements

First, I want to thank all of my grammar and spelling and reading teachers at every educational level for instilling in me a love of words and their use. Also, I want to thank everyone who has heard me use words and encouraged me to continue anyway.

I am indebted to my wife, Roxanne. She is my rock, she is my conscience, she is my friend, she is my sparring partner, and she is the love of my life. She has nearly as many opinions as me.

I offer my thanks to Mother and Dad for being my greatest inspirations. I am among the fortunate few who, in adulthood, found that my parents were also my friends. I also thank Amy and Elizabeth for being my sisters. I love them both, and owe many of my opinions to my relationships with them.

Maria and Cristina are my joys, my challenges, and my compass. When I was old enough to be somebody's grandfather, instead I became their father. While there are days when I try to figure out just what I was thinking, far more often I realize what a wondrous, mysterious experience it is to be the father of daughters.

The people of the Emington Congregational United Church of Christ have been my anchor for nearly eleven years. They have asked very little of me while giving me more than I deserve. I thank God for them every day.

I also want to thank Bobb for being my brother. We were born and raised twin sons of different mothers and, in the fullness of time, our brotherhood was revealed. His love has given me the courage to voice my opinions.

My thanks go to the American Bible Society for providing something to prod me along each day. Having a starting point made things easier.

Finally, I want to thank God. I'm not sure what I mean by that, because I'm not at all certain who God is. I am certain that God knows who I am and has told me so.

Preface

A few years ago, I made one of my trips to the hills of southern Indiana to visit a couple of friends of mine who live back in a holler near Riddle Ridge (Don't strain too hard trying to find it; only the most discriminating maps include it.). These friends are also my momma and daddy. After an active and busy life raising children and working, along with various and sundry other activities, they decided that the peace and quiet of the hills was just too inviting to resist.

During the aforementioned visit, Dad and I were talking about something which was, I'm sure, quite earth shattering. We get into these discussions whenever we are together, mostly just for the fun of the debate. Anyway, he offered his view on the subject, and then said, "Of course, I have an opinion about everything." I didn't give that much thought at the time. Late that night, though, as I was lying in bed listening to the burning wood as it hissed and popped in the stove, I heard him say those words again in my mind. I realized that he was right. I've known the man my entire life, and I truly can't remember a time when or a subject about which he didn't have something to say.

In the time since that fateful evening, I've come to another revelation that is either affirming or disturbing, depending on the day of the week when it is being revealed to me. I am my father's son. I am my teacher's student. I am my mentor's mentee. I am a chip off the proverbial block. I, too, it seems, have an opinion about everything. Some of my opinions have some basis. Most are my opinions just because they are my opinions, and I'm not particularly concerned with whether or not they have any basis.

I am finding that many of my opinions are related to matters religious. This would be because I have devoted a large portion of my personal and professional life to the pursuit of things spiritual. While I have been fairly successful at separating my faith from religion, I *do* fancy myself a disciple of Jesus of Nazareth. As near as I can tell there has never been a wiser, more compassionate, more astute, more spiritual human being than he. My first spiritual realization came as a result of being taught about Jesus and his relationship with God by my Sunday school teachers. I depart from orthodox Christianity, though, in that I cannot worship any God but God and I view as idolatrous attempts to rationalize deifying Jesus.

That being the case, I have some opinions to share about the whole matter. What follows are a very few of my opinions, based on my journey thus far.

TO BEGIN WITH

Once Upon a Time

He began to teach them many things in parables … (Mark 4:2)

Once upon a time …" As a young boy, all my favorite stories started with those four words. I knew that a story was coming that was going to be fun to read or hear, that I would probably learn something and, most importantly, that I would be able to understand the doggone thing. I thought I had died and gone to heaven when my mother and dad bought me a book with nothing in it but Aesop's fables. Every story in that book started out, "Once upon a time." It didn't matter that the stories were make-believe. In fact, that was part of why I liked them so much. The story had to have something outside what I knew to be real to hold my interest. Talking animals, talking plants; the more there were the better the story.

Parables are the same kind of story. They are make-believe. They are figments of someone's creative imagination. But, they teach an important lesson. More than that, they teach in language that is easy to understand. That's why Jesus used parables to do most of his teaching. He was a master story-teller, and he knew how to get a point across. Best of all, he knew how to tell stories using images and ideas that were part of the common, every day existence of the people listening to him.

When it comes to fulfilling my call to share The Story with people, Jesus has always been my role model. I use a simple three-step formula: 1) tell *a* story, 2) tell *The* Story and, 3) relate it all to the *listener's* story. It works. Jesus knew what he was doing.

Once upon a time, an old country boy started telling stories. Somebody needs to shut him up before he gets himself in trouble.

Loud Silence

... suddenly a light from heaven flashed around him. (Saul) fell to the ground and heard a voice ... He asked, "Who are you, Lord?" The reply came, "'I am Jesus ... " (Acts 9:3-5)

Here we have the conversion story by which all other conversion stories are judged. Saul the Pharisee, self-styled Christian-killer, is on his way to carry out a few more dastardly deeds in the name of God. A bright light flashes, Saul falls down, sees that he can't see and hears a voice coming out of nowhere, "Hey, Saul; why are you picking on people who don't believe what you believe?" "Who wants to know?" is Saul's retort. "Jesus," is the reply.

I'm not even going to talk about the possibility that old Saul got struck by lightning and that rendered him temporarily sightless. But, he heard the voice. How he knew that the voice was telling the truth when it identified itself as Jesus, only Saul knows. Nonetheless, he did hear the voice and he did know who it was.

Ever since that fateful day, lots of folks have somehow come to the conclusion that a "blinding light" experience is the only valid experience. No doubt, many people do have dramatic experiences which bring them to the realization that they are in the presence of something or someone almighty and eternal. My dad had such an experience in 1965. It was real, it changed his life immediately, and he's been a disciple, scholar, and teacher ever since. I thank God everyday for Dad's experience.

I, on the other hand, pretended to have one of those experiences that same year because I thought everybody expected it of me. I pretended to be Ed Christian for the next 24 years because I thought people expected it of me. I pretended to be called into the ministry and went to a seminary because I thought people expected it of me. I pretended to be serious about the whole thing and let the church ordain me because I thought people expected it of me. However, after 24 years I felt like the biggest liar the world has ever seen and realized I couldn't pretend anymore. For all those years, I tried to continue being Ed Christian just in case there really was a God; I was hedging my bets. As I say though, I couldn't pretend any more. I walked away from the churches where I was pretending to be their pastor and drove down to Arkansas and sat on the side of a hill for a week listening to nothing (or so I thought.) After a week, I got back in my truck and headed home. I was glancing at a Red Man Chewing Tobacco sign when the thought suddenly struck me that the Arkansas silence had been anything but silent. Sometime during that week of hill-sitting the spirit of God (or whatever the Ultimate Reality is) spoke to my spirit. As my eyes were being enticed to try a chew of Red Man, some other part of me to whom I had never been introduced came to life for the first time. It was a bright, sunny day with no flashing lights; I didn't fall out of my truck; and I wasn't struck blind. It all happened in silence so still that I didn't even realize it happened until it was too late. All I can say with any certainty is that, by the time I got back home, I knew that God is real and had silently told me so. Most disconcerting of all was realizing that I had been chosen.

I'm really happy for Saul, and for my Dad. I'm just as happy for the experience of deafening silence.

What Free Will?

I don't care what people may say about us having to make some choice about or commitment to God. God chooses people to do things that need done. When the time was right, God knocked Saul down with a bolt of lightening, and Ananias followed up by explaining to him, "The God of our ancestors has chosen you." I went and sat on the side of a hill in Arkansas fully expecting to leave as empty as I arrived. Instead, once I left I realized that God had chosen me. I could no more have said "no" to being chosen than anything. I knew, in a way that I can't explain, that I had been chosen and there was no choice left to me. I rather expect that Saul had a similar realization.

So, what happened to free will? What happened to the necessity of "giving your life to God?" "The God of our ancestors has chosen you," almost leads me to believe that Ananias wasn't a good and faithful Jew, but that he was a Calvinist Reformer spouting ideas about predestination. Why, the whole idea is a blasphemy against everything that I was taught is good and Christian and holy.

The truth is, I'm not willing to argue with anybody about the whole free will thing. Intellectually, I'd like to think that people have a choice to make. I simply know that God chose me, and I can't debate that.

Also, not only have I never regretted that God did the choosing, I am relieved. I previously thought I had made a choice, but I wore myself out trying to prove it. Once God chose me, my spiritual life became and remains a source of energy rather than a cause of exhaustion.

ALL IN THE FAMILY

Just Like In the Old Days

"They shall eat the lamb ... roasted over the fire with unleavened bread and bitter herbs." (Exodus 12:8)

When I was about 13 years old or so, I went to a summer "wilderness" camp as it was called. It was one of those deals where we "roughed it," so to speak. We did some of our cooking on an overturned coffee can with a sterno burner for heat. The rest we did by wrapping food in aluminum foil and putting it in the coals of a wood fire, or by putting it on a spit over the fire. We made everything from "scratch," using what was available to us. What we didn't have was salt, or pepper, or nice fluffy loaves of bread in clear, plastic wrappers. After receiving a rudimentary lesson in herbology, we were to find our own seasonings as nature provided them. We were also to make our own bread using flour and water, no yeast. The idea, of course, was to teach us to make do with what we had available. We wound up with roasted meat, unleavened bread, and bitter herbs. I'll never forget that experience, because I learned an important lesson about knowing the difference between what I want and what I need.

So it is, that the instructions for the Israelites in celebrating the Passover were to cook in the way that they did in the wilderness, using not what they wanted but what they had that would meet the need of feeding them. In this way, it became a memorial celebration as it caused the people to hearken back to a time when they did what they had to do to survive and lived to tell about it.

I'm not one for living in the past; it's done and I can't fix it. On the other hand, some stuff happened back there along the way that taught me lessons that have proven to be valuable as I move ahead. Also, there are a few memories that are quite pleasant for me, and it just feels good to remember them.

I always want to be the one to put the ice cream in the egg nog on Christmas Day. It reminds me of Christmas at Grandma Beryl's house. She died in 1997, but the memory lives on, and I do a silly little thing as a tribute to a woman I loved deeply and because the memory is good.

Doing silly things only becomes problematic when doing so ceases to be a tribute to a good memory and, instead, becomes religiously institutionalized, routinized, regulated. Religion has no place among the spiritually faithful.

Scotland, 1576

The time that the Israelites had lived in Egypt was four hundred and thirty years. (Exodus 12:40)

I don't know about you, but I remember the year 1576 just like it was yesterday. Why, Clan Sinclair was having a bonnie good time in the Scottish highlands that year. Farming and hunting and having old-fashioned donnybrooks with all the neighboring clans. All in all, it was a great time to be alive.

That was, as those of you who are adept mathematicians can readily ascertain, four hundred and thirty years ago. Of course, my memory is not that long. The oldest memory I can recall came some three hundred and eighty years after that. I have never been to my ancestral homeland in Scotland. Even though my memories aren't four hundred and thirty years old, and even though I have no clue what Clan Sinclair was up to in 1576, I am, nonetheless, affected by it.

History seems to have a way of progressing in a cause and effect manner, at least the little bit of it that I deem to be truthful. Thus, if I had the time and the inclination, I am quite certain that I could trace my family history back to the Scottish highlands in 1576, and then work my way back in such a way that a picture would emerge that links me, however obscurely, to my ancestors.

The Israelites had been in Egypt for the same number of years—four hundred and thirty. Naturally, not one of them who was alive when Moses went and led them out of there had ever been anywhere but there. It was the only home they knew; it was the only existence they knew. But, for the same reason that I am linked to my ancestral past, they were linked to theirs, as well. While Moses came to disrupt the only life they knew, they were, I'm sure, aware that there was a reason because the stories had been kept alive.

I have said before that I am not one to live in the past. However, there are times when being aware of the past can be quite instructive.

The Faithful Remnant

"But now for a brief moment favor has been shown by the Lord our God, who has left us a remnant, and given us a stake in his holy place ..." (Ezra 9:8)

When I left home in 1971 to seek my place in the world, the country church of which my family had been part for several years was at a zenith. Membership was nearing 200, and worship was regularly attended by 125–130 or more. Things were going well!

After a few years, a pastor came who was a bit different than others the people had come to love and respect. This man had very strange ideas and made even stranger demands upon the church community. He seemed enslaved by a distorted understanding of God's will for his life, and was determined to draw others into his life of spiritual slavery with him. Fairly soon, people began to feel alienated. Not long after, some began to worship elsewhere. By the time the guy had been there for three years, there was but a remnant left; no more than 25 or 30 on any given Sunday. The man was finally removed from his position by the church hierarchy, but the damage was done.

Still, there was a remnant of faithful folk. They held together and remained steadfast in their loyalty to God and to one another. Slowly, they began to pick up the pieces of what once was and started rebuilding it. They realized that God had "given (them) a stake in his holy place."

The Israelites were living in Babylon as spoils of war, and were being used as slaves. But, a man named Cyrus became king of that realm and thought enough was enough. He declared the Israelites free people, and sent them home with his blessing. They went under the guidance of a priest and scribe named Ezra. Though their numbers were no longer great, still they were a remnant. In that small band of still faithful people God saw enough to warrant godly favor and "a stake in his holy place."

Those faithful Israelites, and my friends back home who endured their own slavery and remained steadfast in so doing, are evidence of the power of faith.

Often, it seems like all else has failed and nothing is left *except* faith. When that happens, faith is enough.

The Family Ingathering

"Lift up your eyes and look around; they all gather, they come to you; your sons shall come from far away and your daughters shall be carried on their nurse's arms." (Isaiah 60:4)

The copy of Isaiah I'm reading calls Chapter 60 *The Ingathering of the Dispersed*. That has a familiar ring to me. Let me tell you why.

Grandpa Sinclair died in May of 1990. Sinclairs from all over the Midwestern United States made their way to a little funeral home in Marengo, Indiana to say "goodbye." Afterwards, all those Sinclairs got together at Mother and Dad's place to have supper together. Dad built a fire in the outdoor fire pit and we roasted what seemed like 300 pounds of hot dogs. As we were all sitting around the fire, Dad invited every one of those Sinclairs from all over the place to come back to southern Indiana once a year. The purpose was to create an opportunity and a reason to be in the same place at the same time without the death of a loved one being involved. Apparently, Dad had been thinking on this for a while, because he said, "It will be called the Crawford County Ingathering." There were twelve of those ingatherings before Mother and Dad started to get tired. Every year the makeup of the group was different. Why, before long, the word got out and people who weren't even Sinclairs were showing up with bowls of tater salad. There was an atmosphere of joy and happiness and silliness at those ingatherings that brought a tear to my eye every time. Folks were genuinely glad to be together in the same place. It was good that they had a reason to come from near and far away.

As much as I loved being at the Crawford County Ingatherings, I can't even begin to imagine how the Israelites must have felt knowing that they were going to an ingathering of epic proportions. It was to be so grand, that Third Isaiah has God say that folks who aren't even Israelites will take notice. Some of them will even show up with gifts a whole lot nicer than tater salad.

Sometimes, you *can* go home again.

Look at Me; I'm a Christian!

"Beware of practicing your piety before others ... as the hypocrites do in the synagogues and in the streets so they may be praised by others." (Matthew 6:1-2)

1965 was the year the Sinclairs went to the Methodist church. Mother and I had been going for a while because she had been recruited to be the piano player. She started bugging Dad to go and he finally did along in the spring. One Sunday in May of that year, the preacher did his preaching, and then he did his altar calling, and Dad trotted right on up to the front of the sanctuary. When he got there, standing right next to him was his younger brother (who just happens to also be my uncle), Dave. Now, Uncle Dave was only "Dave" to Aunt Phyllis (who, strangely enough, is his wife). To the rest of us he was, and is, Dink (in my case, of course, that would be Uncle Dink). The reason for his nickname is a story for another day. Anyway, there were Dad and Uncle Dink standing there in the front of the sanctuary wondering what in the world had just happened to them. Not long after that, their little sister (who just happened to also be my aunt) Susie got herself some salvation somewhere; I don't remember where. Before anybody really knew what was happening, there were about three pews full of Sinclairs and their subsidiaries in the sanctuary of the Morris Chapel Methodist Church on Sunday.

In October of 1965, I succumbed to the pressure to join the Sinclairization of that church and got baptized. Didn't seem to change much at the time for me other than people stopped asking me when it was going to happen. Well, I figured if I was going to be one of those Sinclair Christians, I needed to at least look the part. So I dug out the bible that Grandma Beryl gave me for my tenth birthday, and plopped it right on top of the stack of books I carried back and forth to school every day. Everywhere I went that bible was right there in plain sight. I didn't read the thing, but it was there for people to see. My colleagues, classmates, and cohorts took notice just as it had been my plan that they do. A few well-meaning souls told me how nice they thought the bible looked perched there on top of the stack like that. On the other hand, there were others who asked,

"What the (bleep) are you doing with *that* thing?" Of course, I would respond by saying, "Why, I'm one of a new breed of Christians called the Sinclairians." Then I would begin to hope desperately that no one would want to know what in the world I was talking about, because I had no idea what in the world I was talking about. I just knew that it was somehow important that I be seen and identified as the pious, devout young man of spiritual distinction that I was sure I was not. It was all about creating an image, and it was the phoniest thing I have ever done.

There must have been some young Ed Sinclairs wandering the streets during Jesus' day. He didn't mince any words at all; he called them hypocrites. All show and no glow. Further, he warned the folks who had been listening to him talk that carrying their bible on the top of their stack was a worthless endeavor if it was done, not to draw attention to God, but rather to draw attention to the one with a stack with a bible on top.

There are still lots of folks who are in the religious game because of how they believe it makes them look in the eyes of others. Jesus' word of caution still applies I believe: "Beware of practicing your piety before others … as the hypocrites do in the synagogues and in the streets so they may be praised by others."

Can You Keep a Secret?

"See that you say nothing to anyone ... But he went out and began to pro-claim it freely." (Mark 1:44-45)

The absolute most sure-fire way to make sure that someone doesn't keep a secret is to instruct him or her not to say anything to anybody. I'll tell you how I finally learned that lesson. For many years, Maria and Cristina would pester me relentlessly to tell them what I bought as a gift for their mother at Christmas. I would hold out as long as I could and then, in the spirit of the season (at least that's what I told myself), I'd let them in on the secret. In no more than two days at the very most, my wife Roxanne would be joyfully singing, "I know what I'm getting for Christmas." The girls just couldn't keep the secret.

Using whatever means was at his disposal, some would say miraculous means, Jesus helped a man with leprosy get better. Mark doesn't tell us how he did it, only that Jesus chose to do it and it was done. As this was still early in the in the history of Jesus of Nazareth Evangelistic Ministries, Jesus asked the guy to keep what happened just between the two of them. He wasn't yet sure what the reaction would be. Of course, the man kept quiet just long enough to get out of range of Jesus' hearing, and then started telling anybody who would listen. The result was that everybody, their neighbor, and their neighbor's dog, went looking for Jesus to see if he could do something for them. Not that he didn't want to, but there was only one of him and so Mark tells us after that Jesus didn't even go to town anymore. The secret was out and nothing would ever be the same.

Do you think I'll ever again reveal to Maria and Cristina what I bought their mother for Christmas? No, nope, no way, ain't gonna happen. They'll just go tell her.

Hey, Ed; Your Brother Is Looking for You

"Your mother and your brothers are outside, asking for you." He replied, "Who are my mother and my brothers?" (Mark 3:32-33)

My mother delivered her first (and only) son in 1952. As it ultimately turned out, her first (and only) son wound up being me. Three daughters followed in the next eleven years, but no more sons. I left my momma and daddy's home in 1971 to join the United States Air Force. All during the four years I served in the military, I was sustained by the hopeful thought of going back home upon being discharged. Thirty-five years have passed and I haven't gone back home yet. God somehow has always managed to get in the way whenever I give any kind of serious thought to going home.

In one way, this hasn't been a bad thing. What was it someone said about absence making the heart grow fonder? In this case, that's true. Even though I never did make it back home to live, nonetheless, over the years Mother and Dad have become my confidants. Thus, the three or four times per year that I am able to be with them are very special indeed.

In 1979, I moved to Kansas City, Missouri to complete my seminary indoctrination. Soon after arriving, I applied for a position as a member of the youth ministry team at a large Presbyterian Church in Prairie Village, Kansas. While at the interview, I was introduced to a skinny fellow from Iowa named Bobb (yep; he spells it with three b's; only he knows why). As things developed we were both hired by the church, and shared a house for a year which was owned by the church. Over the course of that year, a friendship developed that eventually evolved into brotherhood. Twin sons of different mothers—that would be Bobb and me.

What's the point of all this? Well, in Mark 3:35, Jesus answers his own question when he says, "Whoever does the will of God is my brother and sister and mother." He knew exactly what he was talking about. Bobb has followed God's call into positions of leadership in the United Methodist Church in his native

Iowa. I've done my best to do the same wherever I've wound up over the years. Bobb is my brother just as surely as if we'd both actually had the same parents.

I miss my parents and my sisters very much, and wish I could spend more time with them. However, over the past thirty-five years, God has grown my family exponentially through relationships not unlike the one I share with Bobb.

Who are my mother and brother and sisters? Those who share the will of God with me.

On Being Adopted

"All who are led by the Spirit are children of God ... you have received a spirit of adoption." (Romans 8:14-15)

The concept of adoption is one that is near and dear to me. Not only that, I think adoption is a good idea. There are tens of thousands of children all over the world with no family, no home, and no hope. I believe that there are people who have a family, who have a home, who have hope whom God calls to share with many of those children who have none of these things.

Our oldest daughter, Maria, spent the first nine years of her life in an orphanage in Quito, Ecuador after being abandoned by her birth mother. Her presence in our family has been a joy and a challenge. Our lives are much richer because she has become one of us.

Paul had a good notion working when he used the analogy of adoption in speaking to the disciples of Jesus living in Rome. What do you suppose he meant? I happen to think that he was referring to the fact that Jesus was born as a Jew, lived his life as a Jew, worked primarily to restore the faithfulness of his fellow Jews, and died a Jew. The message which Jesus shared, however, was universal in its applicability. Paul recognized that and devoted his life to sharing the message with folks who weren't Jews. In so doing, he made available to "gentiles" the heritage and teachings which Jesus represented and interpreted so well. In other words, Paul made it possible for all people to be adopted.

Roxanne and I first considered the idea of adoption after my best friend, Bobb, and his wife, Susan, adopted children from Korea. They now have four beautiful children sharing their home, their love, and their name; Roxanne and I are godparents for two of them. Adoption is a good thing. More people ought to consider it.

Welcome?

"Each of us must please our neighbor for the good purpose of building up the neighbor … May the God of steadfastness and encouragement grant you to live in harmony with one another … Welcome one another, therefore, … for the glory of God." (Romans 15:2, 5, 7)

"I'm telling you right now, Reverend, I been a member of this church since 1915 and I don't want none of those Black people in my church, so don't you even think about it! They let some of them people in my aunt's church and they ruined it with their dancin' and hand clappin'."

This was my introduction to parish ministry in 1975. I had just finished my first sermon at the United Methodist Church in an Illinois suburb of St. Louis and was standing by the back door doing my first "meet and greet" with the members of the congregation. The speaker of the above words was a very sweet looking woman who I judged to be somewhere on the other side of 90 years old. But, when she spoke there was strength in her handshake and fire in her eyes.

The community where we were lies just to the north of East St. Louis and had, during this young lady's lifetime undergone a cultural transformation from an exclusively White community to one which had become predominantly Black in terms of racial makeup. I was to find that the lady who gave me my stern warning was speaking the conviction of the majority of the people who frequented the pews of that little United Methodist Church.

I felt as though I had been backed into a corner in which I didn't care to be. I was raised that there is great beauty in all God's children and that diversity should never be feared but celebrated. I made a quick decision, however. I would not make any overt effort to bring Black people into that particular United Methodist Church. Not because I feared any reprisals, but rather because it did not seem to me to be a place where they would want to be.

The members of that church were not bad people; they were the inheritants of a bigotry of such long standing and deep conviction that it was part of their nature and they could not see how it conflicted with what they professed on Sunday morning. When the opportunity presented itself, I never backed down from talking about equality and justice. Mostly, though, I tried to love to the people as I found them.

On the other hand, I spent every free minute down at the playground at the school where several of the young friends I made there taught me the finer points of the game of basketball. I was always the only White player there, but no one seemed to notice or care. In fact, one of the proudest moments of my ministry in that town was the day the young men almost got into an argument over who would get to have "the preacher" on their team.

> *"Each of us must please our neighbor for the good purpose of building up the neighbor ... May the God of steadfastness and encouragement grant you to live in harmony with one another ... Welcome one another, therefore, ... for the glory of God."*

Who Do You Belong To?

… each of you says, "I belong to Paul," or "I belong to Apollos," or "I belong to Cephas," or, "I belong to Christ." (I Corinthians 1:12)

During the second year of my seminary indoctrination, I was told that I needed to align my personal theological perspective with one of the acknowledged "masters" of Christendom. Was I Augustinian? Could it be that I was a Calvinist? Perhaps my leanings were more contemporary. Maybe I was a Tillichian, or a Bartian, or even a Bultmanian. One thing was certain, it was understood that I was not capable of an independent theological thought, and so had to grab onto somebody's coattails in order to have any semblance of credibility.

To begin with, I had read a little bit about what each one of those boys had to say. I agreed with some of it, I disagreed with some of it, and I didn't understand most of it. Every one of them wrote their thoughts in theologianese, a language that was not spoken with any regularity in the hay barns where I worked as a boy. Secondly, I was perplexed as to why I needed a "theological perspective" anyway. It had never occurred to me to want one, let alone need one. The pressure to claim allegiance mounted with each passing day. Finally, in order to put an end to the silliness, I announced that I had come to a decision in the matter. I announced to all who cared to listen that henceforth I would be a Sinclarian. As near as I could tell, the only opinion about my relationship with God that was of any importance to me was my own (and God's, of course). Much to my surprise, I was belittled and berated for being arrogant and unorthodox.

The exact same thing was going on in Corinth. The burning question was "are you a Paulinian, or are you an Appolonian, or maybe a Cephan?" People were getting all upset with each other over whose sermons they liked best. It was to the point that this mattered more to them than being followers of the way described by Jesus. So Paul reminds them that their priorities are a little out of whack.

I think that, just to be on the safe side, I'll proclaim myself a Godian. That ought to keep me out of trouble. On the other hand, I've met a few faithful atheists along the way.

Will the Ushers Please Come Forward?

"Now concerning the collection for the saints; ... I will send any whom you approve with letters to take your gift to Jerusalem." (I Corinthians 16:1, 3)

Back in the late 1800's somebody came up with the idea of paying men to play baseball as a means of creating a recreational diversion for people in a few large cities in the United States. The idea was such a good one that pretty soon other towns wanted to have professional baseball teams, too. That went so well that other towns wanted to have professional baseball teams, too. After a time, a downside to this passion for professional baseball teams began to reveal itself. It became increasingly difficult to come up with enough players with enough talent that people would pay to see them play. This led to someone else coming up with the idea of having "farm teams" or "second level teams" or "feeder teams" or whatever they were called. These teams could play in smaller towns because their main purpose would be to prepare players to play for the larger market teams while not having to pay them as much to play. This would insure that the original teams would be able to continue because there would be a ready pool of new players to draw from. This depiction of the development of minor league baseball may or may not have any basis in fact. I made it up because it suits my purpose.

As far as the early Christian movement was concerned, the original large market "major league" team was in Jerusalem. When Paul was doing his thing, this group still included a couple of charter members, most notably Peter. Jerusalem was still a regional center for the Roman Empire and the Christian movement there was under constant scrutiny, not to mention threat of annihilation. So, meeting basic daily needs was a very tenuous proposition. This being the case, Paul struck a deal with the "big club." He figured that for his work to have any credibility out in the hinterlands, it would be nice if he could say that he had the approval of Pete and the boys in Jerusalem. As part of a clever marketing strategy, the "saints" in Jerusalem would be willing to give Paul the seal of approval as long as he could convince people in the places where he went to tell the story that it

24

would be good if they could pitch in to take care of the original team which was struggling at the box office due to the aforementioned Roman scrutiny/threat. Everybody gets something out of the deal. As a result, history tells us, Paul's work was made a whole lot easier, the movement grew in numbers quickly, and the folks in Jerusalem didn't starve. Sometimes, negotiation and compromise can work out for everybody.

Ah, Kenny Kommanders baseball; it doesn't get any better than that.

I'd Rather Do It My Way

"I am astonished that you are so quickly deserting the one who called you in the grace of Christ and are turning to a different gospel—not that there is another gospel." (Galatians 1:6)

I got myself a banjo not too long ago. I didn't look for anybody to help me learn to play the thing, I just started banging away. The first chance I had, though; I visited with my dad, who has been picking the banjo for at least forty years. I asked him to show me what he knew. So, he sat there for a while patiently showing me some things he had figured out about playing the banjo. Then I tried to repeat what he showed me. It was easier than what I was doing on my own and the banjo sounded better. I came back home and got my banjo out. Within five minutes I was back to trying to play the thing like I had before my visit with Dad.

This scenario plays itself out in the Bible, too. Remember what happened when Moses decided to go camping up on the mountain for a few days? In no time at all, the people were bothering Aaron to build them a god like they were used to. Aaron was happy to oblige and made them a cow out of their melted down jewelry. It happened again in the region of Galatia. Paul had come through there and spent some time with the folks in these towns telling them his story and sharing how getting acquainted with Jesus had a profound effect on him. Before you know it, he had meetings going in several of the little towns there and everything was peachy keen. Then came that time when Paul decided to move on and tell the story to some more folks on down the road. After a while, people started bringing some of their old artifacts to meeting with them and, before you know it, they had some sort of gobble-de-gook conglomeration going on there but they were still calling it Christianity. Not only that, just to prove that absence makes the heart grow fonder, they start questioning Paul's credentials since he wasn't ordained.

One of my many bones of contention with organized religion is about this very thing. Somehow or another, the notion has taken root that, while God may call people to serve in some way, it's the church that ordains them. I'm not about to buy that for even a minute. I started this "professional ministry" business thirty years ago in a branch of organized religion that insisted that people weren't really ordained until the church had ordained them twice! They ordained you once just to see if you were serious and then did it again a few years later after you had *convinced* them you were serious. Of the many true ministers of God I've known in my life, very few of them had a stamp of approval from some church. But ... every one of them was ordained by God to do what they were doing. Paul was no different.

I find it kind of interesting that Christians claim a Jewish layman as their Lord and Messiah, and that it was a man who intentionally walked away from his life as a Pharisee who took the message all over two continents. Make no mistake; they were both ordained by God, no matter what the church said.

Who in God's Name?

"… I bow my knees before (God), from whom every family in heaven and on earth takes its name." (Ephesians 3:14-15)

What's in a name? I guess that depends on who you're asking. Where do the doggone things come from? They come from everywhere, it would seem. I know that I was given the name of my dad's closet high school friend. It honored that man, and it has given me a two-letter nick name that is easy to spell. I looked it up one time and found out that my name (Edward; though nobody calls me that) originated in England and means "Royal Guardian." Sounds kind of official, doesn't it?

Then there's the only professional football team worth mentioning in print. Of course, I'm referring to the Green Bay Packers. The name of this legendary franchise pays honor to the hardworking folks who for decades have made their living in the packing houses of that fair city. I could go on, but I hope you get my point. Names almost always mean something significant to somebody.

What do you suppose that Paul means when he starts his prayer for the Ephesians by saying that everybody living and dead is named after God? Well, the thing is, another one of those strange habits that religious people have is naming themselves after some predecessor or another. The Lutherans take their name from Martin Luther. The Calvinists, who have since spun off in several directions, took their name from John Calvin. As a group, the Christians have taken their name from Jesus Christian (or at least that's what many seem to think). An important part of Jewish heritage has been tracing their lineage to Abraham.

I get the feeling that Paul is intimating here that none of us climb far enough down the family tree to find out where the whole name thing actually started. Our name as children of the Creator comes, not from Luther, not from Calvin, not from Jesus. Our name can be traced all the way back to the Creator. To stop anywhere short of that is to take upon ourselves a false name.

Lovey Dovey

"… This is my prayer, that your love may overflow more and more with knowledge and full insight to help you determine what is best." (Philippians 1:9-10)

It's just nigh on to impossible to avoid this whole love thing if you spend very much time reading the Bible. It lurks around every corner, just waiting to jump out and embrace everybody. In this letter to the people at Philippi, Paul throws in a couple of attributes with which he would like love to come equipped: knowledge and insight.

Love seems to totter about blindly most of the time, at least in many of its everyday expressions. I heard somebody say the other day that they loved cooked turnips. Now, you and I both know there is something incongruous in *that* image. Then there are people who say, "I love you," and it comes with an unspoken caveat: "as long as there is something in it for me."

Paul was no dummy; he was well aware of how folks threw love around loosely. So, he tells the Philippians that he is praying that their love will be based on knowledge and insight. Particularly, when people start talking about loving other people based on their relationship with God as it has been revealed to them through teachings about Jesus, Paul wants to make sure they have the story straight. "Educate yourselves," he said. "Gather up whatever insight (or wisdom) you can," he encouraged. "Base your love on what you learn," he suggested.

How much aggravation and irritation do you suppose could be avoided if love, that most illogical and irrational of all emotions, could actually have some basis in knowledge and wisdom? "Do I love you? Do I love you, you ask? Let me come to know you; let me develop significant insight and wisdom concerning you. Then, in the fullness of time, I might come to feel affection akin to love for you." Doesn't that just seem infinitely logical and practical? I love it!

On the Outside Looking In

"Conduct yourselves wisely toward outsiders, making the most of the opportunity." (Colossians 4:5)

In February of 1992, I was a true outsider for the first time in my life. Roxanne and I traveled to Ecuador to meet the little girl destined to become our daughter and to do the legal work necessary to make that a reality. Roxanne had traveled outside the United States several times before; I had not. Not only was I traveling to a foreign country for the first time, I was going to a place where the language spoken was other than my own. As we stepped onto the tarmac at the Quito airport, I was greeted with a chorus of, "¡Hola!" "¡Buenos noches!" Man, was I glad I had studied a little bit of Spanish back in high school!

For the next two weeks, Roxanne and I were about the only English-speaking people with whom we came in contact. Further, as we were among people who had lived their entire lives within fifteen miles of the Equator, we were, by far, the most fair-skinned people we saw. However, we were also treated graciously and courteously by every person we met. As I have indicated, we were obviously outsiders. We were strangers in a land we found quite strange. None the less, to use Paul's words, the Ecuadorians treated us wisely and made the most of the opportunity to form friendships with us. I hope I can get back down there for a visit some day.

On the other hand, have you ever met any good and faithful Christians who are a little stand-offish when new folks come to Sunday meeting? There's something about strangers that makes us get our hackles up, isn't there? How sad it is to think that there are people out there in the world who came to visit looking for a friendly face and a warm smile, yet were treated with suspicion instead. They didn't find anything inside the church house that was very inviting. That happens far too often I think. It seems to me that there are some opportunities of which not much is made.

We Are Family

"The one who sanctifies and those who sanctify all have one God … Therefore he had to become like his brothers and sisters in every respect." (Hebrews 2:13, 17)

I am fortunate that I have reached this stage of my journey through life with the notion that whoever I am should be someone of whom my parents can be proud. The same holds true in terms of my relationship with God. I want to be a son in whom God can take pride.

I'll tell you what; the author of this treatise will do whatever it takes to make a point, even if what he does is as confusing as all get out. In Chapter 2, he or she continues to compare and contrast angels with human beings or, more specifically in this instance, Jesus. We find out that, according to the theological musings of our author, Jesus gained his eternal legitimacy as a sanctifier by willingly assuming a status somewhat lower than the angels (that is, he was a human being). As a result of his having assumed such status and then living out and ultimately ending that status as he did, he proved his true place in the eternal hierarchy which, as it so happens, is somewhat *higher* than the angels.

I don't know if what I just said makes any sense to you at all. It makes my head tired just thinking about it. However, the author makes a relational connection that interests me. He makes the point that, as a human being, Jesus was a brother to all other human beings. First of all, this shows that the author had a true vision of how the human community should function; like family. Secondly, though, if Jesus was thought to be the son of God, and if all other human beings were his brothers and sisters, doesn't that imply that all his brothers in the human family were also sons of God, and that all his sisters were daughters of God?

I suppose some may find that notion blasphemous since everyone knows that God only has one offspring. The fact remains that the author of Hebrews reminds us that not only was Jesus not God's only offspring but every human being from the first until now can rightly claim God as eternal parent.

I really don't care whether or not God likes angels more than God likes me.

Are You Serious?

"Be serious and discipline yourselves ... Above all, maintain constant love for one another, for love covers a multitude of sins." (I Peter 4:7-8)

Today is the anniversary of my birth. Fifty-four years ago my parents brought forth their only begotten son. Not only am I their only begotten son; I am the first of their offspring. Thus, I suppose I was their child-rearing guinea pig. I clearly recall that my upbringing had its fair share of seriousness. Also, discipline was swift and, all in all, fair. It would also be truthful to say that through it all they maintained constant love for me and any parental miscues were covered by that love.

The author of I Peter utters these words because he or she is convinced that the end of human history is at hand. The tone of the writing indicates that this person was quite concerned that people be ready for the bench trial which Jewish history and tradition insist is the fate of every person at the end of his or her life. It just would not be right or proper for people to be having a ripping good time when the end comes. Meeting the Maker is serious business and preparation for this meeting must be serious and disciplined.

I beg to differ! Every morning when I walk into the bathroom and look at that guy on the other side of the mirror, I am convinced once again that God has an unbelievable sense of humor. God laughs out loud with great regularity, I just know it. God wants us to be able to laugh, too.

More than that, God wants us to love one another. I don't know about you, but it is very difficult for me to love seriously. Loving people just feels too good to get all serious about it. So ... I must respectfully disagree with the author of this epistle. As a matter of fact, when it is time for me to set aside this weather-beaten form, I want to be playing a guitar or a banjo, or maybe a game of croquet, or laughing at a good joke.

No doubt about it, I want to head into eternity laughing my silly head off.

GETTING HEALED UP

On the Bottom, Looking Up

"My spirit is broken; my days are extinct, the grave is ready for me … My days are past, my plans are broken off …" (Job 17:1, 11)

During the time that I worked in the world of mental health, my strongest feelings were always evoked for those folk who were on the bottom rung of their mental ladder and could find no reason to think that they might be able to climb to the second rung, let alone to the top. They could find nothing to which to hold fast. They had no lifeline. They had no hope. They had no faith. That has to feel completely desolate. I confess that I've had a few desolate moments of my own. It's not an experience I recommend.

On a lighter note, do you remember this little grade school tune?

"Nobody likes me, everybody hates me;
Guess I'll go eat worms.
Fat ones, skinny one, gushy ones, squishy ones;
Worms that squirm and squirm."

Who among us has not sung that lively refrain at some time during our childhood? Don't you just love the vivid imagery that it uses to express the feelings of someone in the throes of self-pity, self-loathing or, at worst, depression? Some of us who fancied ourselves musical even figured out how to sing the song as a round.

Of course, the reality of which the song speaks, and which Job experienced, is nothing at which to laugh. Job was so low because of his circumstances that he began looking to death as his only possible source of relief. Anything that could go wrong for him did go wrong. Everything he held dear was taken from him. His friends abandoned him. As the author of his story states, Job's spirit was broken, he could foresee no future for himself, and he was ready to die. Job had lost everything with one exception. When everything else was gone, when everyone else was gone, Job held tightly to faith. Faith was his only lifeline. He clearly got plenty mad at God for his predicament. After all, in his day and time, the belief

35

was that if your life went down the drain it was because you had offended God; you had sinned, and God was getting you back. The thing was, Job had pretty much walked a straight, narrow line based on his relationship with God, and bad stuff happened anyway. When all was said and done, though, Job refused to believe that God was totally to blame for his situation. When nothing else was left and his hope jar was all but empty, he swiped down around in the bottom with his spatula and came up with a little bit of faith. That little bit was enough to sustain him.

I'm not going to lie to you for a minute; I'm not nearly as strong as Job. I need more than what he had to sustain me.

Goodness Gracious, God is Good

"I believe I shall see the goodness of the Lord in the land of the living."
(Psalm 27:13)

The other day, I saw a robin. Not a big deal, I suppose. To me, though, it's a *very* big deal. When the robins start showing up here in the part of the world where I live, it's a sure sign that spring won't be far behind. Never mind that it snowed four inches yesterday and the schools were closed. I saw that robin, by golly, and spring is coming! For me, robins are quite definitely a sign of God's goodness here in the land of the living. I've survived another winter, of which I am not at all fond, and the temperatures are moderating, trees will bud before long, life will explode into being as it does each spring.

I went to a bluegrass music festival not long ago. "You went where?" you may well be wondering. I went to a bluegrass music festival. All acoustic music; nothing electric. Guitars, banjos, mandolins, fiddles, all being played to produce the purest music of which I am aware. It's not everybody's cup of tea, for sure. But it certainly is mine. At this particular festival, at one point an older gentleman came out followed by about ten young people, the oldest of which may have been twelve years old. Each of these young folks carried either a fiddle, or a mandolin, or a banjo. It turns out that the gentleman on the stage with them has dedicated a significant portion of his time to teaching youngsters how to play bluegrass music on the various instruments. Not a big deal, I suppose. To me, though, it's a *very* big deal. The hair stood straight up on the back of my neck as I watched those young'ns sawing and picking and strumming away. Any time someone will take the time to share a gift with others that they might know it and enjoy it as well, that is quite definitely a sign of God's goodness here in the land of the living.

The fact is, God's goodness is all around us and it's mostly in simple things like robins and youngsters learning bluegrass (or Beethoven, for that matter). We need to make sure we're not looking for God to do something spectacular; we might miss the spectacular things God is doing.

Here, Piggy Piggy!

Those who saw what had happened to the man and to the swine ... began
to beg Jesus to leave their neighborhood. (Mark 5:16-17)

I've always had trouble with this story about Jesus and the guy filled with a whole legion's worth of demons. I'm not bothered by the description of the demons; that's a great way to describe somebody's behavior when we don't understand it. I'm not bothered by the fact that Jesus chose to help the fellow out. I'm not bothered by the fact that the man wanted to tag along afterward, nor am I bothered by the fact that Jesus told him to go home and tell the story there instead. You want to know what bothers me? The pigs. I just can't get those pigs out of my mind. First of all, what were they doing there? Even on the other side of the river, most of the people were Jews or of Jewish descent. Everyone knows how kosher pigs are. So, I want to know why they were there. The thing is I can't find anybody who can answer that question for me to my satisfaction. Then there's the conversation between Jesus and the demons. They beg him not to send them out of the area, but ask if they could maybe possess the pigs instead. With a response that one might expect of a faithful Jew who always looked for the kosher "K" on packages at the grocery store, Jesus says, "Sure, go ahead." Then the third thing that troubles me happens. As soon as the demons take up their new residence, the pigs go running off down the hill and into the sea where they drown. Were the demons really stupid, or did they know this would happen? Even if those pigs (Mark says 2,000 of them!) weren't fit to eat, they were still God's critters, and it doesn't quite seem fair to me to treat them that way. After all, no matter why they were there, there must have been a legitimate reason. The story also tells that there were people called swineherds who had the job of looking after them. They watched their livelihood run off down the hill and into the sea. All in all, I'm happy for the guy who Jesus cleaned up but how were these folks supposed to make a living now?

There is no real moral to these meanderings. I just feel really bad for the pigs.

Faith is the Victory

Now there was a woman who had been suffering from hemorrhages for twelve years. She had endured much under many physicians, and had spent all that she had; and she was no better, but rather grew worse. She had heard about Jesus, and came up behind him in the crowd and touched his cloak … Immediately her hemorrhage stopped and she felt in her body that she was healed of her disease. (Mark 5:25-29)

When I was eight years old, Mother and Dad took me to the hospital on the day after Memorial Day to have my tonsils taken out. No big deal; kids do it all the time. Later on I got to eat ice cream like other kids do. The next day I went home like other kids do. The next day I started spitting up blood like other kids don't. I wound up back in the hospital where all kinds of doctors spent the next two weeks trying to keep me from bleeding to death. I'm writing this 45 years later, so I guess they got it done.

In 1991, I had some corrective surgery. No big deal; people do it all the time. Later that day, I went home like other folks do. That night I developed a high fever. I wound up back in the hospital where it was discovered that I was hemorrhaging on the inside. It turns out that I have von Willebrand's disease, and my blood doesn't clot right. I found a blood doctor (I think they call them hematologists) and he fixed me right up. The disease isn't cured, but I know how to take care of it so it won't cause me so much aggravation.

I tell you this to let you know that I can empathize with this woman. She had been bleeding off and on for twelve years. The doctors couldn't figure out how to help her; appropriate chemotherapy hadn't been thought of yet. She had spent everything in her 401(k) plan trying to get some help, and now she was broke. So, figuring she had nothing left to lose, she snuck up behind Jesus and touched the clothes he was wearing. Near as I can tell, Jesus never did anything. She touched his clothes and the bleeding stopped. It had everything to do with what she did and why she did it.

Jesus looked at her and told her that it was *her* faith that made her well. He didn't do anything; God didn't do anything. But she had faith in something, and it made her well.

There are all kinds of stories about people who are beyond what medical know-how can do for them, but get over it. Jaded doctor after jaded doctor says the same thing: it is faith in something bigger than medicine that makes the difference.

Faith—such a simple little word with such incredible ramifications.

Don't Mess With Mamma

"Sir, even the dogs under the table eat the children's crumbs." (Mark 7:28)

You talk about stubbornness; you talk about audacity! The person who smarted off to Jesus about dogs and crumbs was a non-Jewish woman who had a sick daughter. Didn't she know any better? What was she thinking saying such a thing to a man who had been working pretty hard to convince his own people to get right with their God?

Jesus and the disciples are up in the Tyre area when this confrontation occurs. They're walking along, minding their own business when a woman comes up and starts to pester and nag poor old Jesus. She must have been pretty desperate, don't you think? Well, knowing that the disciples (and some of the woman's neighbors) were watching, Jesus makes a production out of implying that his fellow Jews were first and foremost in God's pecking order. But this is a mother with a sick child. She's not about to put up with any nonsense. When Jesus says something about feeding the children first rather than throwing the food to the dogs, she makes her retort which according to the Ed Sinclair Version was, "You know how children are; they're messy, always dropping crumbs on the floor. Who eats those crumbs? Why, what do you know, the dogs do!"

Now, I'm guessing that is exactly what Jesus was hoping she would say because it gave him an opportunity to begin showing his faithful Jewish disciples and those Gentile neighbors that God was just too big to be confined to being only the God of one group of people. By the woman talking back and saying, in so many words, "I want some of what you have, too; Jesus," he was given the opportunity to say, "Alright, you can have some. Go on home, your daughter is well."

Hey, I eat crumbs all the time; best part of the whole meal.

Spit—The All-Purpose Cleaner

... When (Jesus) had put saliva on his eyes and laid his hands on him, he asked him, "Can you see anything?" (Mark 8:23)

Do you have one of those mothers who thinks spit is the ultimate, all-purpose cleaner? I sure do. It's not so bad if they rub a little on you at home when no one is looking to make you presentable for inclusion at the evening meal. But, *my* mother took her greatest delight in taking out her handkerchief, spitting on it, and then rubbing all the skin off my face right in the middle of the grocery store, or at the ice cream stand, or, worse yet, in the school parking lot with all my fellow scholars in attendance for the ritual cleansing. What *is* the fascination with spit?

All I know is, it must be pretty good stuff! Mark tells this story about Jesus using a little of it to correct a man's vision problem. As with most of the stories he tells, Mark doesn't go into any great details about the situation other than to tell us that Jesus and the boys were in Bethsaida and they were met by some folks who wanted to introduce their sight-impaired friend to Jesus. After the obligatory, "Hi, I'm Fred. Hi, I'm Jesus," Mark says Jesus put saliva (we all know it was spit) on the guy's eyes, laid hands on him and asked him if he could see. I also find it kind of interesting that the man's first response was, "Well, I can see a little, but nothing to write home about." So, Jesus does it again. It took two tries. I've always wondered about that. I guess I'll have to wait a while to get a straight answer.

After the man finally tells Jesus he can see well enough to know what he's looking at, Jesus does something at which he had become quite adept. He told the guy not to say anything to anybody. Now, I suppose there could be a couple reasons for that. Maybe he figured it would be a little embarrassing for the man to walk up to his friends, and say, "Guess what? I can see!" only to have them say, "How did you manage that?" Would you want to try to explain somebody spitting in *your* eyes and make it sound like a good thing? More likely the real reason was that Jesus knew what the repercussions would be if there continued to be more and more stories about the neat things he was doing for people. He didn't

42

yet want to deal with those repercussions and, besides, being the truly humble person he was, he saw no reason to brag or to have someone else brag for him. He was just doing what he understood God wanted him to do.

Oh, yeah; my mother loved to use spit to smear down my cow licks, too. That's just plain gross!

SOME LESSONS
LEARNED

Covenants—Who Needs 'Em?

God spoke to Moses and said to him, "I appeared to Abraham, Isaac, and Jacob; I also established my covenant with them." (Exodus 6:2-4)

I was going to school in Ohio when I promised Grandpa Thomas that I would make a trip to Indiana to sing at the church he attended. We made all the arrangements, I practiced diligently, and then I was hired to begin a new job that ultimately prevented me from keeping my promise to Grandpa. I struggled mightily with my dilemma; I truly wanted to do what I had made the promise to do, and I really needed to accept the job in order to cover expenses for the upcoming school year. My need for the income ultimately outweighed my commitment to keep my promise. I called Grandpa and explained my predicament. He was gracious and very understanding of the situation. Nonetheless, I felt as though I had committed an act of betrayal.

The thing is I was raised with the notion that a person's word is the deepest and most final commitment a person can make. "Don't make a promise you can't keep," I was told time after time. I have always tried to heed that advice because I don't ever want my word to be considered unreliable.

In Exodus 6, God is still getting Moses ready to go get the home folks out of Egypt, and Moses is still complaining about his self-perceived inadequacies. God counters the unrelenting series of "yes, buts" that Moses is coming up with by saying, "Look, I made a promise. In fact, I made that promise to three consecutive generations of the family of Abraham. Believe me when I say that I keep my promises." Actually, what God has done goes even beyond the every day, garden variety promise. God made a covenant. My understanding of covenants is that they are generally considered to be legally binding agreements. Now, I don't suppose that God would be very concerned about the legality of any agreements God has made. However, I would very definitely suppose that God would consider such agreements binding. That being the case, we can rest assured that God will be bound by and will fulfill the terms of any covenant God enters into.

I have often heard Dad say that the only way he can not be bound by a promise he has made to someone is to be released from the promise by that person. I have concluded that he (and God) enters into covenants, not promises.

It's OK, 'Cause God Said So

If a man has sexual relations with a woman who is a slave, designated for another man but not ransomed or given her freedom … an inquiry will be held since she has not been freed. The priest shall make atonement for him, and he shall be forgiven. (Leviticus 19:20, 22)

In this chapter of Leviticus, we find a slightly different version of Exodus 20 which, of course, contains what history has named The Ten Commandments. I, however, was intrigued by verses 20-22 which I have edited liberally above. Here we find God handing down a very interesting command. If a man has sex with a female slave, it will be looked into, the priest will say a couple prayers and kill a couple sheep and we'll all go down to Joe's for a beer. This is to be the case even if other arrangements have been made for the woman's future welfare. As long as the man still has the title and registration (and proof of insurance, of course), having sex with her is not the best thing to do, but it is apparently not all that bad either.

I highlight this "commandment" by way of saying that I certainly hope all those people who say that God "wrote" the Bible, that it is without error and is, in fact, infallible never stumble across my musings and have the book's considerable fallibility brought to their attention. I can just see it now. The scene takes place down at the First Church of the Human Condition. "But, pastor, it says right there in Leviticus that not only can I own women and make them slaves, I can even have sex with them and God says it will be alright if I tell you about it and you kill a sheep. I even brought along a couple of young rams for you. Got 'em out in the back of the truck."

With all due respect and deference to my biblically literal brethren and sistern, this is a reflection of a different time and culture. This is no commandment of God. God would not have people owning people. God would not have women looked at as the property of men (or vice versa). All people are equal in God's eyes. There aren't enough wacky priests or young rams in the world to change that. Besides, let me remind you of something. Leviticus 19:17 says, "… you shall love your neighbor as yourself."

There Are Aliens Among Us

"Any alien residing among you who wishes to keep the passover to the Lord shall do so according to the statute of the passover and according to its regulation; you shall have one statute for both the resident alien and the native."
(Numbers 9:14)

In one community where I was a pastor, almost all of the men were members of a national fraternal organization. The second or third week I was there, one of the prominent members of the community stopped by my house to get acquainted, or so I thought. After about five minutes, he asked me if I were already a member of the fraternal organization. I had never been part of, nor seen any need to be part of, any fraternal organization and I relayed this, nicely of course, to my guest. "Well," he said, "Every pastor that has ever lived in this town has been a member of the fraternal organization." He then shoved a membership application at me and told me he would be by the next day to pick it up once I had completed it. To this day, I'm not sure which part of, "Gosh, I don't care," he failed to comprehend.

Later that day, when I had a free minute, I picked up the application out of bored curiosity and gave it a cursory glance. Almost immediately, the most interesting thing jumped out at me. About half way through, there was a sentence with options for circling "yes" or "no" at its conclusion. The sentence stated:

"I hereby certify that I am of pure, white blood.   Yes   No"

This presented me with three immediate difficulties. 1) My blood is red; 2) I cannot state with absolute certainty that my European ancestry has been untouched by other ancestries and; 3) how dare someone boldly attempt to badger me into taking a blatantly racist, prejudiced, discriminatory stand such as this? I was being asked to swear my allegiance to something that would purposely exclude others. When Mr. Fraternal came back the next day, I handed him back the blank form and said, simply, "I can't say that I'm of pure, white blood." He took little time making his exit.

How unlike my experience is the direction supposedly given by God regarding who can and cannot take part in the Passover meal and ceremony. *"Any alien residing among you who wishes to keep the Passover to the Lord shall do so."* Short, sweet, and to the point. The observance is open to all, regardless of what kind of blood they have or don't have. No ifs, ands or buts. To drive home the point, the author of the Book of Numbers has God giving this directive. Notice, if you will that the statement uses the word "shall" rather than the word "may." In other words, no permission is necessary; the feast and what follows are accessible to every person who chooses to participate.

Just try walking into some churches of which I am aware and ask for a piece of bread and some grape juice. If you don't have a particular stamp of approval on your forehead, they will look at you like you are some sort of a whacked out reprobate and refuse you the courtesy of sharing their repast.

I don't know about you, but this sort of ecclesiastical exclusivity just doesn't sound much like a good example of the compassion and generosity God would have people to show to one another.

Something is screwed up, royally.

Does God Really Drive a Mercedes?

"When you have eaten your fill and have built fine houses and live in them, and when your herds and flocks have multiplied, and your silver and gold is multiplied, then do not exalt yourself, forgetting the Lord your God, who brought you out of the land of Egypt." (Deuteronomy 8:12-14)

If you haven't figured it out by now, I'm a country boy and right proud of that heritage. Imagine my surprise then, when I was asked invited to be part of the "ministry team" at a church that had over 7,000 members. This church is located in Johnson County, Kansas which at the time of my experience had the second highest median income in the United States. The church had 85 full and part-time employees. I was invited to be one of six youth ministers. On any given Sunday evening, about 150 to 175 young people would show up for the youth fellowship meeting. They came in Corvettes and Porches and Camaros and Mustangs and Mercedes. Did I mention that these weren't their parents' cars? These were the cars that parents had purchased and given to their teenaged sons and daughters.

The year I spent there was a truly eye-opening time in my life. I had never been in the presence of wealth before. I had seen the word "opulence" in a book somewhere, but had never witnessed the reality. There were many good and faithful people among that throng of 7,000. However, I clearly remember God and faith taking a back seat to the prestige of being a member of the church. It was the church where the powerful people went to be seen. Members of the Kansas City Royals baseball team took their babies there to be baptized. Politicians liked how being a member of the church made their resumes look. Religion (not faith) was very much on sale there and no price was too high. There was no end to the available financial resources. I came away from that experience having the very clear thought that, as a group, that church had seen its flocks and herds and gold and silver multiply, had exalted themselves for a job well done, and had forgotten who brought them out of the land of Egypt.

Wealth in and of itself is not a bad thing. It can be a blessing for some who know that possessing it gives them a responsibility to use it to create more wealth that can be shared. Possessing wealth can be detrimental, however, when it becomes god or when it gives people the false sense that they can either buy themselves a god or create one to their liking. There's no amount of wealth that will, in the final analysis, ever be able to bring anybody out of the land of Egypt.

I'll Scratch Your Back …

"O Lord God of heaven … let Your ear be attentive and Your eyes open to hear the prayer of Your servant that I now pray day and night before You for Your servants, the people of Israel." (Nehemiah 1:5-6)

I can't even begin to count up the number of letters of reference I've been asked to write over the years, or that I have requested be written on my behalf. Maybe you've written a few of these little epistles as well. Usually, the person requesting such a letter is either seeking employment, admission to an institution of higher learning, or something of that sort.

"Mr. Sinclair, I'm making application for admission to the freshman class at Upper Northern University of the Southwest and was wondering if you could write a letter to the Dean of Admissions which attests to my academic successes, extra-curricular involvement, and daily teeth-brushing regimen." "Ed, I'm applying for a job at Silent Sam's Sofas and Fast Lube. Would you write Sam a letter telling him how conscientious I am, that I never lay on my couch and I change the oil in my car every 2,500 miles?"

I admit that I sometimes enjoy singing the praises of a requester when I feel those praises are well deserved. I have no difficulty speaking on his or her behalf. Why, there are even times when I might shine a light on somebody without them even asking if I think doing so is warranted and would be helpful.

Nehemiah found himself doing this latter thing. He was still up in Susa which was one of the capitals of the Persian Empire. He was aware that Cyrus had sent Israelite folks back home. The first chance he had to ask somebody, Nehemiah was anxious to hear how things were going back in Jerusalem. The word he received was not particularly positive or promising. This being the case, he chose to speak to God on their behalf, even though the home folks hadn't asked him to do so, nor were they aware that he was doing so. It was the right thing to do, and Nehemiah did it. It didn't much matter to him if the people he was speaking for knew anything about it or not.

How often do you have the opportunity to speak on someone's behalf? Maybe you're not asked to write reference letters very often, but I'll bet you have opportunities every day to speak to God for the sake of somebody. I guess I don't figure it hurts to take advantage of those opportunities when they come about. I sure don't think it matters whether anybody knows you did it except you and God.

Truth Be Told

"… they bless with their mouths, but inwardly they curse." (Psalm 62:4)

This psalm reminds me of Eddie Haskell. You remember Eddie Haskell, don't you? He, Wally Cleaver and some guy named Lumpy made up the hormone-driven teenage triumvirate on "Leave It to Beaver." When ever Eddie would come to the Cleaver's house, he really turned on the charm with Mother Cleaver. "Yes, Mrs. Cleaver," "You're looking lovely today, Mrs. Cleaver." She thought Eddie was just about the greatest young man in town (other than Wally and the Beaver, of course). But, as soon as he was out of earshot, Eddie was about the most obnoxious, ill-mannered dude you've ever seen.

While I love everybody because I believe God expects that of me, I don't like the Eddie Haskells of this world. I can handle anybody who looks me in the eye and speaks their truth to me, no matter how offensive, repugnant, or strange I may find their truth to be. But those folks who smile their fake smiles and say things they think I want to hear and then tell anybody what a dope I am when they think I can't hear them makes me go running for the antacid. Who do they think they are fooling?

Just tell me the truth. I'm a big boy; I can handle whatever you throw at me as long as it is the truth. To use David's word, anything else is a curse to your integrity and mine.

I'm a Light Sleeper

"When I ... meditate on You in the watches of the night ... my soul clings to You." (Psalm 63:6, 8)

I am a light sleeper. I wake up at the slightest noise or movement near me. I guess that's why I get to take the dog out in the middle of the night. Everybody else in the house knows I'm the one who will wake up. The dog even knows. He doesn't even bark. He just crawls out from under the bed and gives himself one good shake. I hear his fur fluffing in the nighttime stillness and off we go.

Not only am I a light sleeper, I experience what I believe to be far too many nights when I sleep little if at all. My head just won't shut off no matter what I do. The off switch gets stuck and there's not enough WD-40 in the world to loosen it up. I try reading; I try listening to a little bluegrass music; I get up and go to the bathroom whether I have a legitimate reason to do so or not. Sometimes, one of these time-tested strategies fulfills its intended function and I lose consciousness for a while. But there are other times when sleep is not going to be part of my experience under any circumstances. I wind up laying there listening to the steady, even breathing of my spouse as she slumbers, and I get jealous. The next thing I know, I've dredged up some memory either good or bad. I either enjoy it for a moment or relive the nonsense all over again. For a lot of years, I would find myself trying desperately to prove myself the equal of one of those philosophers like Hume, or Kant, or Bishop Berkley; all of whom spent their lives in an impossible pursuit. They thought they could logically prove the existence of God. I would lay there at night trying to come up with some mental construct or another that would convince me, once and for all, that God really is. Of course, my efforts were as fruitless and futile as were those of my philosophical predecessors. God cannot be proven.

But then, I had an experience when God spoke to my spirit and made all my previous efforts irrelevant. I still have my nights when sleep is not on the menu. The thing is now what I find myself thinking about is how incredible it is that God chose to be revealed to a life-long, committed skeptic like me. That is a very comforting thing to think about when I'm not sleeping.

Besides, and I know I'm going to offend somebody when I say this; I wasted my time pondering that philosophy stuff, because it is nothing more than mental gymnastics that quickly dissolves into the excrement of the male of the bovine species.

Praise Oak from Which All Blessings Flow

"The carpenter … cuts down an oak (and) it can be used as fuel. Part of it he takes and warms himself; he kindles a fire and bakes bread. Then he makes a god and worships it, makes it a carved image and bows down before it." (Isaiah 44:14-15)

As hard as it may be to believe, I do some really stupid things from time to time. I'm not talking run-of-the-mill everyday stupid things; I'm talking industrial strength, prime grade stupid things. How and why this happens I haven't a clue. However, it is a skill which I have, over the years, honed and refined and practiced with no little abandon. If I have the good fortune of succumbing to one of my bouts of stupidity while in the presence of my loving spouse, her considered and well-thought-out retort is really quite consistent. In her gentle, loving voice she will say, "Ed, you are such a knot-head!"

I've often pondered what it means to be a knot-head, but I've not had the courage or the need to make serious inquiry. Sometimes I think that perhaps she is suggesting that I've sustained some sort of cranial injury the swelling and bruising of which is impairing my highly developed capacity for logic and reason. But then there are other times, when I get this mental picture of my head looking like an old piece of firewood with a big old hollow knot in it. Not good for much except splitting and using for stove wood.

Second Isaiah is making fun of some of the weird worship practices people have been coming up with during their captivity. He mentions a carpenter. The guy cuts himself down a nice tree to burn in the stoves (cooking and heating). But, he saves the piece with the big old hollow know in it, carves a smiley face, and then proceeds to worship it. Yeah; can you imagine that? Worshipping a piece of stove wood like it was some sort of god. That's just the height of silliness, don't you think?

Well it's no sillier than people who worship the church pew they've sat in for 50 years, or song books they use that came over on the Mayflower. It's sure no more silly than people who make their money or their possessions their god. Strange doings, that.

I've got an old bicycle tube out in the shed with a hole in it. I'll bet I could make a right nice god out of that. Better yet, there's a big rock next to the mailbox; now that's a god just waiting to be worshipped.

In Your Dreams!

"No more shall there be an infant that lives but a few days, or an old person who does not live out a lifetime; one who dies at a hundred years will be considered a youth." (Isaiah 65:20)

I was watching TV in my seventh grade classroom in 1964. There were what seemed like millions and millions of people standing outside in Washington, D.C. A man walked up to the microphone and said, "I have a dream …" He went on to talk about his dream; a dream where people are seen and understood as people, period. Not green people or orange people or purple people or skinny people or fat people; simply as people. I remember that day 42 years ago like it was yesterday. The man's dream hasn't come true yet. But, because of his efforts and the efforts of others who share his dream, in some instances the way people view one another is slowly evolving for the better.

As the Israelites made their way back home, Third Isaiah shared his dream with them. They were leaving behind the certainty of slavery and were headed toward the uncertainty of freedom. They must have been filled with a mixture of absolute joy and striking fear. By way of bolstering their resolve, Third Isaiah says, "Once we get home, I have a dream that we will multiply in numbers and live a very long time. I have a dream that we won't have to bury so many of our babies and we will live long enough to truly make a difference." The truth is Third Isaiah's dream hasn't come true yet. But, because he and others like him were bold enough to share the dream, people have been catching a glimpse of it ever since, and the world has been a better place as a result.

The human race needs all the dreamers it can get.

Hey! Let's Blame God!

"Why has the Lord pronounced all this great evil against us? What is our iniquity? What is the sin that we have committed against the Lord, our God? ... Because you have behaved worse than your ancestors, for here you are, every one of you, following your stubborn evil will, refusing to listen to me." (Jeremiah 16:10, 12)

Back in those thrilling days of yesteryear, it was very common for folks to think that, when calamity struck, it was because they had done something to make God, or the gods, or whoever angry. It's a theme that replays itself in many religious traditions. Have a drought and the corn doesn't grow; we better figure out what we did to get on the bad side of the rain god. Get overrun by a superpower like Babylon and be carried off as slaves; you made God mad, you made God *really* mad.

Jeremiah lived and worked in the kingdom of Judah. The time and events described in these words attributed to him are just after Israel has already been conquered and the people taken away and a similar fate is fast approaching Judah. All over the place, people are wondering, "What did *we* do?" In the marketplace, the conversation is about seeking an answer to that question. Down at the temple, the sermons are attempts to come up with an answer to that question. At the Monday night meeting of Jehovah Lodge #587, same thing: "What did we do?"

As I said, it was the common line of reasoning that when bad things happen, it's because God is angry. According to the legend, Jeremiah is the one who has the unenviable task of providing the answer to the question. "It's all quite simple, really," he says, "Your behavior is bad, you are quite stubbornly choosing to pursue evil rather than goodness and, worst of all, you won't listen when God tries to talk to you."

There you have it. The Babylonians are coming because the Judeans created a few idols to worship. Exile and slavery are imminent because they have turned their attention away from God and have become lawless.

Is that really why the Babylonians were able to accomplish what they accomplished? I don't know; I have not yet made the acquaintance of anyone who was there at the time. Logic would say that Babylon was successful because they *could be* successful. What Jeremiah said to the people surely gave them something to think about.

I don't believe that God is out to get people just because they lose focus. Further, I don't believe that God sets out to punish people who do things we may not like. I don't care what anybody thinks; men and women are not dying in faraway wars because God doesn't like gay people. Hurricanes and tornadoes don't devastate entire areas of the country because God thinks we should have eaten beef instead of pork for supper last Thursday. But; folks just have to have somebody to blame for things and a reason to blame them and a way to make it look like it's God's idea.

We must really give God a pain in the posterior with all this nonsense.

Come Together, Right Now

"We have heard a cry of panic, of terror, and no peace … Can a man bear a child? Why then do I see every man with his hands on his loins like a woman in labor?" (Jeremiah 30:5-6)

Art had just celebrated his 80th birthday. About a week after the blessed event, he found out that he had cancer of the prostate. Further, he was told that his prostate would have to be removed. On the day of the surgery, I was at the hospital with his wife, Leila, and one of their daughters, whose name I no longer remember. The prostate was successfully removed and Art was, for the moment at least, cancer-free.

After he was moved from the recovery area to a regular room at the hospital, his daughter and I went in to see him. He was awake, though not totally alert. His daughter said, "How are you doing, Dad?" Art moaned for a moment, and then indicated that his pain level was somewhere around 14 on a scale of 1 to 10. His daughter then said what I thought was really cruel. She said, "I think God gave old men prostrate problems since they can't give birth!" It took me a moment to gauge the relationship between father and daughter and realize that this was good-natured banter. The idea of a man giving birth conjures up all kinds of freaky images, doesn't it?

Speaking on behalf of God Almighty, Lord of heaven and earth, Jeremiah has just informed the exiles that God is getting ready to bring them home. And, as an added bonus, when they get home they will be one people, one kingdom again. Now, you would think that the thought of going home would be cause for great rejoicing. Instead, there is bellyaching and whining and complaining. In fact, there is so much moaning and groaning going on that God is given the impression that the men all think they're having babies. If the impending events weren't so momentous, the image would be down right humorous.

This scenario reminds me of trying to get small children to take medicine. Even though they know it's good for them; even though they know they will feel better, still they fight and kick and lock their jaws so that they won't have to ingest the pharmaceutical. It's not what they're used to; it's not something that can be located in their vast storehouse of knowledge and experience.

So it is with the exiles. Israel and Judea have been separated long enough that there probably aren't any folks alive who remember when Israel was one nation. They had either always been Judeans or Israelites, and never the twain had met in their experience. Now, they are being told that their respective national and cultural identities will be wiped out once they return home. They do not seem enthralled by the news they are receiving. Sometimes, whether a thing is good or bad depends very much on the history of the individuals experiencing whatever the thing is.

Crick Fishin'

Then Jonah prayed to the Lord his God from the belly of the fish ... Then the Lord spoke to the fish, and it spewed Jonah out upon the dry land. (Jonah 2:1, 10)

When I was about 8 years old, Dad and I went crick fishin'. Or more properly stated we tried our hand at angling in Hummel Creek. The only thing was, there was nothing proper about that day as I recall; so I recollect that we went crick fishin'.

Things were going along just fine, I'll have you know. Truth be told, we had snuck on down the crick a little ways and were back behind Earl Garrison's place. We were sitting on the bank, cane poles in hand, and were bonding as only a father and son can do while watching their bobbers sitting serenely on the glass-like surface of the stream. All of a sudden, my bobber wasn't there any more. I looked everywhere and couldn't find it. Then, my cane pole jumped right out of my hands all by itself. Did I mention that it had rained the night before and the bank was slicker than grease on a hog on the Fourth of July? Just in case I didn't, it had rained the night before and the bank was slicker than grease on a hog on the Fourth of July. I made a desperate lung for my pole and slid down that bank just as gracefully as a guy stealing home plate in the bottom of the ninth inning. When I went to sliding, so did Dad as he made a noble attempt to prevent me from crossing home plate, er; I mean before I went into the crick. We both managed to dampen our already muddied lower extremities just a bit. Meanwhile, I grabbed hold of that cane pole, hung on for dear life, and the dadburned thing broke right in two. Dad and I grabbed hold of the top piece and started pulling on it as we clamored back up the bank. When we got up to the top, we looked back and lying about half way up the bank was the bobber I thought I'd lost. Casting our gaze even further back down the bank, right at the edge of the water was a carp about ten feet long that must have weighed about 300 pounds. It was wallowing my hook around in its mouth like a little person with a mouthful of mush. Dad and I sat there gazing in awe at this amazing aquatic specimen. When we finally caught our breath, I looked back down just as that fish winked at me, spit out the hook and lazily swam away.

Now, what does that tale have to do with Jonah? Quite a lot, actually. They are two of the biggest fish stories ever told. Don't get me wrong; everything I told you about that fish I caught was true except for him winking at me. I had to throw that part in to make the story better. The Jonah story makes for good telling, too. God gives him a job, Jonah says, "Not in *this* lifetime," and runs as fast as he can the other direction. So, God decides to have some fun. Along comes a carp a whole lot bigger than the one I caught and released, and swallows Jonah whole. Interestingly enough, the fish's gastronomic process seems to have no affect on Jonah. Instead of getting digested, he sits there and begins to pray to God. Well, when Jonah refuses to become the proper nutrition for the fish and it starts getting really bad indigestion, God takes pity on the fish. It swims up to the nearest bank, and to use the biblical description, it "spewed Jonah forth on the dry ground." I don't know about you but, where I live, when somebody spews, it is not something to be discussed over tea and crumpets. It's nasty and disgusting. I imagine Jonah was nasty and disgusting when that fish spewed him forth.

It just goes to show that when God has a job of work for you to do, you might just as well do it and be done with it. Otherwise, you might get spewed forth by something somewhere.

Don't Get Above Your Raisin'

"Look at the proud! Their spirit is not right in them; but the righteous shall live by their faith." (Habakkuk 2:4)

"Pride goes before a fall." "Don't break your arm patting yourself on the back." Don't get above your raisin'."

I've had every one of these platitudes directed my way over the years. Pride seems to be considered something of a vice no matter what centuries find pride being purveyed within their chronological confines. When I was younger and Dad would talk to me about the relative futility of trying to reach behind myself far enough to pat my own back, I thought he was telling me that *any* pride was an unpardonable offense against all that is holy.

I don't think that is what Habakkuk was referring to when he made his comment about the proud. I'm pretty certain that he was referring to those folks who genuinely wear their pride on their sleeves. They exist to be noticed; they need to be the center of attention in any situation. They don't understand why everyone around them doesn't automatically look up to them in awe and admiration. That kind of pride is downright scary. I don't think anybody is that important, under any circumstances, at any time. Habakkuk goes so far as to say, "Their spirit is not right in them." In other words, the truly proud have distorted priorities and an overwhelming sense of their own importance. They have no time for righteous living; they are far too busy considering what situation is out there that must have their input in order to enter the realm of legitimacy.

On the other hand, contrived humility is just as bad. In my mind there is nothing more shallow than a person who presents himself or herself as humble and unassuming to the rest of the world because it is to her or his advantage to do so. In the end, I think Habakkuk would most likely group these folks together with the truly and outwardly proud.

That leaves us with the righteous, and I do believe there are a few of these folks. I even think I might have met one or two of them in my lifetime. These are the people who, for whatever fortuitous reason, have realized that every good gift they have and can share comes from God and it is God who should get the credit.

They know that they are channels through which blessings can flow and that they are not the source of the blessings. Finally, it is this fortunate few who live by their faith in Someone greater than they. Sadly, the righteous seem to be few and far between.

What Gives?

"Though the fig tree does not blossom, and no fruit is on the vines; though the produce of the olive fails and the fields yield no food; though the flock is cut off from the fold and there is no herd in the stalls, yet I will rejoice in the Lord; I will exult in the God of my salvation. God, the Lord, is my strength."
(Habakkuk 3:17-19)

Habakkuk has been run through the mill. First, he complains to God because the home folks are not behaving themselves. Then, God reassures Habakkuk that the Babylonians will be used to take care of the situation. Now, Habakkuk is looking around at the aftermath of it all. There aren't any figs, there's no olive oil, the fields are barren, and there are no sheep or cattle left. In other words, everything that is essential for the survival of the people has been destroyed. There's just nothing left to speak of.

In many times and many places, many people find themselves in pretty much the same situation as Habakkuk. For whatever reason(s), everything that is important is either taken away or has become inaccessible. To be able to climb back up to the bottom would be a significant achievement. When this happens, it seems to me that folks have three choices. One, they can give in to the despair they are feeling and be consumed by it. Two, they can try valiantly, but ultimately vainly, to climb out of the hole on their own initiative. Or three, they can do what Habakkuk chooses to do. They can come to the realization that, no matter what their circumstance, they are not alone. God is with them. God is the lifeline. Though creation as they know it has crumbled, the Creator remains unchanged.

I can tell you that number three is often the hardest to accomplish, but it offers the most reassurance. More than one time in my short little earthly experiment, I have been at the point where God was what I had left. Sometimes I've had to force myself, but I say "I will rejoice in the Lord; I will exult in the God of my salvation. God, the Lord, is my strength." When it gets right down to it, as long as I can rejoice in the Lord, things will be alright.

It's Just a Building ... Isn't It?

The word of the Lord came by the prophet Haggai saying, "Who is left among you that saw this house in its former glory? How does it look to you now? Is not in your sight as nothing? ... The latter splendor of this house shall be greater than the former, and in this place I will give prosperity." (Haggai 2:1, 3, 9)

It seems that some religious communities have a misplaced sense of priority when it comes to the grandeur (or lack of same) of the edifice in which they gather. 10,000 member congregations build 10 million dollar buildings in which they spend their 12 million dollar annual budget while starving people live in cardboard boxes two blocks away. I know I'm strange, but I can't shake the feeling that there is something askew about those scenarios.

On the other hand, in a local newspaper last week there was a story about a small, but strong community of faith in a rural area near here whose 125-year-old building burned to the ground. The fire was discovered by a member of the congregation who happened to drive past the building on his way home for lunch and saw the flames. When interviewed, the man spoke as though a member of his family had died. Out in the country where I have chosen to live and work for most of my life, the church house is a vital part of the landscape in every community. People who aren't officially affiliated with the congregation and who don't even bother to go to Easter worship are, nonetheless, very quick to speak fondly of the church house and its importance to the community. Thus, I'm quite sure that a member of the abovementioned man's family *did* burn to the ground and die the other day.

The prophet Haggai appears quite briefly on the scene as the people of Israel are mourning just such a death. Haggai's prophetic utterings occur soon after the people have been released from captivity in Babylon and have gone home to see what is left. One of the first things they notice is that the church house has not survived. However, Zerubbabel, the Persian-appointed governor, makes haste to see that a place of worship is constructed with all due dispatch. The people are glad to see that the rebuilding of the temple is a top priority in the reconstruction effort. However, once the building is complete, it is not the same majestic building it was built to replace. Rather than express their thanks that they have been provided with a place to worship so soon after their return, they are disappointed because it's not the same; it's just not the same. For a while, they seem to have adopted a similar the-size-and-impressive-nature-of-the-building-is-more-important-than-the-reason-the-building-exists-in-the-first-place syndrome as their counterparts some 2,500 years later. Speaking for God, Haggai makes them aware of their short-sightedness and encourages them to hang in there and be faithful. The best is yet to come; that is God's promise.

I wish Haggai could pay a visit to that little community whose church house burned down the other day. I'm guessing they could use the same kind of encouragement he gave to the people of Israel.

Pick Me! Pick Me!

He appointed twelve to be with him, and to be sent out to proclaim the message. (Mark 3:14)

My youngest daughter, Cristina, lives, eats, breathes and sleeps volleyball. She has played the game at every conceivable level for the past four years. She goes to volleyball camp in the summer. I constantly have to remind her not to practice her overhand serve in her bedroom (the inventory of broken items is becoming quite extensive.). She was a member of the 6th grade varsity team. She was a member of the 7th grade varsity team. She went to tryouts for the 8th grade varsity team but was not one of the twelve girls picked to represent the school on the team. She was understandably upset.

Being picked for the team is important to our ego and sense of well-being, don't you think? We believe that it means we have been found worthy; that we're "good enough." Sometimes, though, the choices made by the coach don't seem to make much sense.

Jesus made some really strange choices when he picked his twelve-person team. He picked a guy named Simon who couldn't keep his foot out of his mouth no matter how hard he tried. He picked a guy named Matthew who worked for the occupying government. He picked another guy named Simon (two Simons; no wonder he renamed one of them Peter!). This second Simon was a member of a street gang called the Zealots and carried a dagger under his robe with which to kill a Roman. I could go on. But the thing is, he didn't pick his team members based on how faithful they were, or on how skillful they were as public speakers, or on the number of days per week they spent in fasting and prayer. He looked for and found something more important. They were teachable; they were trainable. Sometimes those are the most critical qualities a member of a team can possess.

Of course, some of Jesus' greatest disciples turned out to be people he didn't pick for the team. They believed in the mission just as passionately, though, and did everything they could to further it along.

Cristina is already making plans for the upcoming volleyball season. She'll do a good job, I think.

You Want Mustard With That?

"With what can we compare the kingdom of God? ... it is like a mustard seed ..." (Mark 4:30-31)

The church whose ministry I have shared for the last ten years had its annual meeting today. I suppose most churches do this in one way or another. The folks get together and talk about what they did last year, look forward to what they might be able to do this year, elect some officers, decide on a budget. All in all, pretty standard stuff. Well, while we were looking back, somebody brought up the party we had in July of 2005 during which we celebrated the 100th anniversary of the building in which we worship. The idea for the party came from a church member who recently retired after a career in education and has chosen to become more closely involved in the church's life and ministry. Bob came to the church council in the spring and said he had an idea for a celebration. He and his spouse would be willing to take the lead in making the idea reality. At the time, the members of the council thought it was a good idea, gave it their blessing, and wished Bob the best. Sort of like encouraging him to plant his mustard seed, I guess. He and his spouse did extensive planning and preparatory work in advance of the celebration.

When the day in July finally came, the celebration was a huge success. People came to party with us who hadn't been to the church in many years. Wow, what a good time we had! Bob's seed had grown into a really big bush! As it was winding down, a woman who introduced herself as Ginny came up to me and said, "Hi, I'm Ginny; and I've come home."

Ginny shared that she had been involved in the life of the congregation many years ago, but had not been back for a long time. She said that as she spent the day with old friends and in a familiar place, she realized that something had been missing in her life and the fellowship of our little congregation was it. In the time since, she has become a warm, loving, and vital member of our fellowship. I view her return to us a little like the birds that come to rest in the shade of the mustard bush.

You just never know what's going to happen when you plant a seed.

Save Those Leftovers!

Those who had eaten the loaves numbered five thousand men (plus the women and children). (Mark 6:44)

I don't care what anybody says, chicken and noodles are going to taste better tomorrow than they did today. Now, don't get me wrong. Chicken and noodles are always good. But once they've become leftovers, they're just better. I think it must be a law of physics or something.

People just love to read and hear and tell this Bible story and make it out to be one of Jesus' most incredible miracles. I don't know one way or another. I don't get too excited about miracles, though. I see this story and think about what it doesn't say. It tells us about the sack lunch one young man brought along. It doesn't mention what the other five or so thousand were carrying in their parfleches. It seems to me that it could well be that Jesus may have taken what the boy had, blessed it, and then everybody else brought out their lunch, too, and before you know it they're having the biggest potluck in history. Like I say I don't know.

To focus on the eating aspect of the story is to miss the most important part, I think. This is a story about leftovers. "They took up twelve baskets full of broken pieces." (Mark 6:42). What did they do with those leftovers? Did they throw them in the lake and feed the fish? Most likely not. I think they probably took the remains of their abundance and shared it with their neighbors who wouldn't have eaten at all that day otherwise.

Next time we get ready to throw out the leftovers, I think we ought to fill a basket first. Don't *even* think about throwing out the chicken and noodles.

God Speaks Medieval English

"You abandon the commandment of God and hold to human tradition."
(Mark 7:8)

"Ed, surely you know that God did not inspire scripture until it was translated into the King James English version. And surely you know that every attempt to retranslate scripture into something other than the King James English version is an abomination."

Yes, friends and neighbors, someone really *did* say that to me. Now, I don't want to offend anybody who likes all those "thee's" and "thou's", but I think there's something a little bit off the beam with what my friend sayeth. I'm not sure I comprehend the spiritual rationale behind coming to a conclusion that one translation of scripture has somehow received the God's Housekeeping Seal of Approval, and all the others have not. More than that, I really don't understand how such a conclusion could become a foundational, even essential, element of one's theological perspective.

I guess it's sort of like folks who sit in the same pew for fifty years, or insist that we keep using those hundred-year old song books because Aunt Ethel's great-grandma donated them to the church. Or maybe it's like some church groups who say they love everybody and everybody is welcome, but ... if somebody doesn't meet their definition of righteous, then they can't assume positions of leadership. Or maybe it's like that guy in "Fiddler on the Roof" who keeps singing, "Tradition! Tradition!"

Hasn't anybody paid attention to the criticism Jesus applies here in Mark? How is it that we still cling so tightly to our traditions even if they are in opposition to God's commandments? Those folks Jesus was talking to wanted to argue about the right way to wash your hands, for Pete's sake! Two thousand years later, we're still trying to argue with one another about what's most right and holy.

I figure if throw on a little soap and water before I pick up my New Revised Standard Version or before I write a new song of praise to God, that's good enough.

Why Would Anybody Want to Rebuke Me?

Peter took (Jesus) aside and began to rebuke him. But … he rebuked Peter.
(Mark 8:32-33)

If there is one thing in this world that I really dislike it's being rebuked. I suppose there are times when I really deserve a good, old-fashioned rebuking. But there are other times when somebody decides to rebuke all over me for reasons of quite questionable justification. The one rebuking that I have no tolerance for is the one where somebody decides I'm a liar and says so.

I will admit that I have many shortcomings, failings, inadequacies, and other assorted imperfections. However, I don't lie. Don't get me wrong, when I'm telling a good story, I may use a little story-teller's license to make the story better. But I don't lie and my feathers tend to ruffle in an unsightly way when I am so accused.

In the short little quote from Mark 8 with which I began this epistle, Jesus has just told the disciples for the first time what he figures the conclusion of his ministry will be. What he shares has what can only be called a dark and foreboding tone. He no more than gets it said when Peter/Cephas/the Rock pulls him over and basically calls him a liar. Mark says that Pete "rebuked him." What Mark means is that Peter called him a liar. Surely three years on the road won't end up as nasty as what Jesus predicts; he must be wrong and Peter accuses him of being wrong. Well, Jesus is having none of that, so he rebukes Peter right back! Jesus even goes so far as to call the guy who he has tabbed to be the foundation of the church "Satan." That's really hitting below the belt don't you think? No matter; Jesus didn't lie and Peter needed to understand that if he were to truly be "the Rock." Peter was thinking too concretely and Jesus needed him to do some thinking of a bit more spiritual nature.

I wonder if anybody has ever been buked prior to being rebuked. Actually, I don't want to know.

Passion ... But For What?

"Let the little children come to me; do not stop them: for it is to such as these that the (realm) of God belongs." (Mark 10:14)

In a fairly large Midwestern town a theatrical production takes place every spring called "the Passion Play." As you might guess, it is a song and dance rendition of the last week of Jesus' life. Folks practice for months leading up to the presentations of this magnificent spectacle. What a wonderful thing to commemorate a life well lived and a sacrifice unimaginable.

I wouldn't go to "the Passion Play" for all the money in all the banks in all the countries of the world. In fact, I can't conceive of any factor that would convince me to attend "the Passion Play." How can I, a crusty old country parson, have such an attitude, you ask? The answer to that question is an easy one. I once received a copy of the brochure advertising the event. The brochure touted the spiritual significance of the event and also specifically excluded anyone under the age of 11. That's right; there in black and white it stated that if you haven't yet achieved your eleventh birthday, then by policy you are not welcome to witness "the Passion Play." The brochure explained that children under this age aren't sufficiently mature and might prove to be disruptive to others in attendance.

As sportscaster Keith Jackson would say, "Whoa, Nelly!" I just got plain indignant when I read that. "The Passion Play" couldn't possibly be about any Jesus of which I'd ever heard. The Jesus with whom I've become fairly well acquainted over the years not only didn't exclude the little people, he said that we'd best be like those little ones because it's folks like them who fit best in God's scheme of things.

I think that the absolute worst thing that can ever happen to a human being is to somehow grow out of their childlikeness. Phooey! Who wants to be an adult? Not me!

In Celebration of Losing the Race

"… whoever wishes to become great among you must be your servant, and whoever wishes to be first among you must be (servant) of all." (Mark 10:43)

My oldest daughter, Maria, lives with a developmental exceptionality. She has never let it stand in her way or slow her down. When it was time for her to begin high school, Mike, the cross country coach (who is a family friend) came to Maria's mother and me and asked if it would be alright for him to invite Maria to be on the team. I must admit that our first thought was, "What's he thinking?" Maria is a native of Ecuador, is of Incan descent, stands four feet, nine inches tall (maybe), and has the shortest legs you've ever seen. Mike saw the looks of skepticism in our eyes and so he shared that his intention was to involve her in a small community of students that would be supportive of her. So we agreed to his experiment.

Maria ran on the team for four years. She finished last in every race but one over the course of those four years. However, she was, by far, the most popular member of the cross country team during those years. She was popular because of her enthusiasm, her dedication to the sport (she ran at least two inches off those already short legs), and her loyalty to her teammates, her coach, and her school. At the end of her senior season, Maria was awarded her "letter" in cross country. Obviously, it was not because of her outstanding ability as a runner. No; it was for those aforementioned qualities. She was joyously last for her entire career, but finished first in the eyes of her coach and teammates.

Now, I'm not bragging or anything. I am *too* bragging because I'm proud of my daughter. But the point is we live in a society that puts far too much emphasis on winning; on being first when there is not a real understanding of what is truly required to achieve that lofty status. As Jesus pointed out to his young followers, James and John, to become spiritually and emotionally first a person needs to know what it is to be willing to put everyone else first in the other spheres of existence.

Do you think I'd ever try to run a three-mile cross country race, let alone finish the fool thing? Not on your life.

A New Day is Dawning

Then they brought the colt to Jesus …; and he sat on it … Then he entered Jerusalem and went into the temple, and when he had looked around at everything, as it was already late, he went out to Bethany with the twelve. (Mark 11:7, 11)

I love to go camping. Now, I'll be the first to admit that I haven't engaged in this particular passion of mine for a while. Somehow or another, I wound up with a beautiful wife and two beautiful daughters for whom roughing it is staying at a cheap motel because the pool is outside. Oh, sweet memories!

The best part of camping is morning. I like to get up a little before sunrise, stir up the coals from last night's fire, put a fresh pot of coffee on to boil, drop in a couple of eggs to settle the grounds and, with first cup in hand, listen to whatever sounds the woods has to offer that time of day, while gazing off to the East to watch the sun rise (at least it rises in the East *most* mornings). That's just about the most peaceful way to start a new day I can think of!

Jesus is facing the start of something new, too. Not just a new day; but a new course of action that will end in his death. It's not going to be all that peaceful, either. The way Mark tells it, up until now, Jesus has gone about his business in a most quiet and unassuming way. Every time he has done something out of the ordinary, he has insisted on silence about the matter. He has entered and left towns unobtrusively. Even so, people have crowded him, hounded him, chased him down, and lay in wait for him; all because they thought he could do something for them. Many times he gave them what they sought, but always with the caution, "Tell no one."

That's all about to change. The time has come and now is for him to confront destiny face to face. So … he sure enough will start to do things differently.

The man had more courage than I'll ever be able to muster up.

God is Not God of the Dead

"As for the dead being raised, have you not read in the book of Moses, in the story about the bush, how God said to him, 'I am the God of Abraham, the God of Isaac, and the God of Jacob?' (God) is not God of the dead but of the living." (Mark 12:26-27)

Some of the folks who spent inordinate amounts of time pondering God's cosmos and their place in it were referred to as the Sadducees. Unlike their counterparts the Pharisees, these folks could find no basis for a belief in any sort of resurrection. Even so, they were aware of the old Torah stories. One of those stories said that if a fellow died and had a brother, his brother was obligated to marry the widow and carry on the family line with her. So, the Sadducees ask Jesus, "What happens if the man has seven brothers, each of whom die one at a time after having married the man's widow. Finally, having run out of brothers to marry, the widow dies, too. At the resurrection, to whom will she be married?"

Jesus responds with the verses I quoted up yonder. The way he figured it, if people were thinking about what happens after you die, they were doing a discredit to God. "God is not God of the dead," Jesus states. "God is God of the living." In other words, they were asking the wrong question. He had told them that once somebody dies, human made rules about who marries who no longer apply. Then, he makes this statement which could lead us to one of two conclusions. First, if the true essence of a human being is the soul and if we can agree that the soul is somehow made of more long lasting stuff than the body it rides around in, then talking about resurrection is illogical and irrelevant. If the soul never dies, then there is nothing to resurrect. Second, why would anyone want to return to this pitiful existence once the soul has been liberated for eternity? Once again, resurrection, it seems, doesn't make much sense, at least to Jesus.

Either way, God's focus is on life; not death. Our focus should be exactly the same. So many people spend their time wistfully longing for the "sweet by and by" that they miss opportunity after opportunity to live as God would have them live. In so doing, I really believe they miss the whole point of what God is about, and of what Jesus taught.

God is God of the living, not of the dead.

Don't Tell Me Who My Neighbors Are!

"You shall love your neighbor as yourself." (Mark 12:31)

If what Jesus says is right, Jerry Stone is my neighbor. Jerry's the guy who I cussed at in fifth grade after he pushed me down and I got grass stains on my brand new blue jeans and I had to go home and explain to my mamma why my new blue jeans had grass stains on them and she didn't want to hear about Jerry Stone because she didn't know Jerry Stone's mamma and so couldn't call her to talk about it.

For being such an often quoted little sentence, this one is just full of assumptions, quicksand, and landmines. Allow me to elucidate.

Assumption 1:	You know what love is.
Assumption 2:	You actually love yourself.
Assumption 3:	You have a neighbor
Assumption 4:	You know who your neighbor is.
Quicksand 1:	Maybe you don't know what love is.
Quicksand 2:	Maybe you don't know how to love yourself.
Quicksand 3:	Maybe you think you don't have a neighbor.
Quicksand 4:	Maybe you've never made your neighbor's acquaintance.
Landmine 1:	You don't want to be bothered with love.
Landmine 2:	You really don't like yourself.
Landmine 3:	You don't want any neighbors.
Landmine 4:	If you have neighbors, you don't like them.

Do you see what I mean? One little sentence and I've come up with twelve potential best-selling book theses right off the bat.

You may be surprised to know that I have an opinion about this little sentence which is part of the great commandment which was passed down for centuries to Jesus by his ancestors in the faith and which has been passed along over the course of many more centuries to us.

My opinion is that this commandment isn't about you, it isn't about love, and it isn't about loving yourself. This commandment is about your neighbor. That's right; your neighbor. Please refer to Assumptions 3 and 4, Quicksand 3 and 4, and Landmines 3 and 4 above.

This is only the beginning of my considered opinion on this weighty matter. It is also my opinion that most people have a very narrow understanding of the word neighbor. It's pretty easy to say, "Sure, I like Bill. He just lives two houses away, but he leaves me alone and that's the mark of a good neighbor." It's equally easy to say, "Let me tell you something about that worthless Jack next door. He borrowed my automatic card shuffler six months ago and I haven't seen it since." Here we have the very typical view of our neighbors. They're close enough to smile at, wave at, yell at, and snarl at.

My opinion becomes even further opinionated because I am quite sure that the original author of this commandment had a far broader understanding of who are encompassed by the word neighbor. My opinionated opinion is even more opinionated than that because I am almost certain that Jesus had the broadest possible view of the meaning of neighbor.

At another place in the story, he expounds on his understanding of neighbor at some length. I'm of the opinion that Jesus would say that every one of us has five billion or so neighbors. There are some troubling implications to that understanding of neighbor. If Jesus is right, Sadam Hussein is my neighbor. If Jesus is right, Osama Bin Laden is my neighbor. In my opinion, the point of this whole thing is that our neighbors are all the members of the human family and we are commanded to love every one of them. Now, I will grant you that there may be one or two that we don't like very much, but that's irrelevant. For no other reason than that God made them, we have to love them.

Lord, help me; Pat Robertson is my neighbor.

Why Waste the Ointment?

A woman came with an alabaster jar of very costly ointment of nard, and she broke open the jar and poured the ointment on (Jesus') head. But some were there who said to one another in anger, "Why was the ointment wasted in this way?" (Mark 14:34)

Roger Perling was the principal of the elementary school in a town where I used to live. Roger was a really good principal. He was also very active throughout the community and just happened to go to the same church as I did. Roger's passion was the game of tennis. He constantly looked for someone with whom to play the game. Roger's skill at the game was nearly the equal of his passion for it. I, on the other hand, as a tennis player made a really good barber. I had an old racket that I had paid $10.00 for back in the early 1970's, but I had never done anything other than just bounce tennis balls back and forth with one friend or another in a decidedly noncompetitive manner.

Imagine then, if you will, my surprise and confusion when Roger stopped by my house one evening and said he had something he wanted to give me. He pulled a tennis racket out of its sleeve. It was obvious even to my untrained eye, that this was not only a tennis racket, this was a *tennis* racket. As Roger handed it to me, he said, "Not that it matters, but this is a $450.00 racket that I hand-strung for you." Being the intelligent and reasonably verbose person that I am, I responded with, "Why?" To which he replied, "Because I like you. Now, meet me at the school gym tomorrow night at 7:30."

When a few people that I knew at the time noticed the tennis racket being prominently displayed at my house, they made inquiries. "But, Ed, you don't even play tennis." One of them said, "I'll bet you could sell that thing and get enough money to pay for the new P.A. system in the sanctuary." I replied, "I'll bet you're right; but I'm not going to do that."

Roger decided that the best way to let me know that he held me in some sort of positive regard was to share something with me that was of great value to him. He wasn't sure how else to let me know how he felt, so he did what he could. I can't play tennis anymore. That tennis racket remains one of my most prized possessions.

The woman did the only thing she could think of to show Jesus how she felt. She knew she had to do something, so she did it. After she did it, the other people who were there said to Jesus, "I'll bet we could have sold what she just poured on your head and got enough money to pay for the new P.A. system in the sanctuary."

Jesus responded by saying that because of the simple thing which the woman did she would be remembered throughout the world. If I have anything to say about it, all the Roger Perlings of the world will be remembered for their simple acts of kindness and friendship.

Going AWOL

Jesus said to them, "You will all become deserters." (Mark 14:27)

Christians just love to hate Judas. After all, there's a conflicted guy in every story. There's always that one character who is not really one of the bad guys, but he or she is portrayed as not being quite as fine or upstanding as she or he might reasonably be expected to be. On the other hand, this character always plays a crucially important role in the story line. Judas is that person in this story. And, like I said, Christians love to hate him.

What my good Christian sisters and brothers seem to overlook is that of the twelve people who had worked and lived with Jesus, Judas is the only one who did not shirk his responsibility in the scheme of things. Unlike Peter, Judas never denied that he knew Jesus. In fact, he made a point of letting people know that he *did* know Jesus. Ironically, because Judas did *not* deny Jesus, people despise him.

For the story to play out as it did, someone had to play the role of Judas. He fulfilled his role in the plan. Where were the others? AWOL. They were, as Jesus accurately predicted, deserters. In most instances, deserters are not looked upon with favor. In fact, they are thought to be cowards or weaklings. Not *these* eleven hombres. Christians regularly sing their praises. Peter, who flat out lied, is revered worldwide to this day. The church in Rome where the Pope is pastor is named after this bald-faced liar. Over the years, I've heard sermon after sermon and Sunday School lesson after Sunday School lesson extolling the virtues of these eleven men who should have been court-martialed for dereliction of duty in the face of enemy fire. Why, they are all referred to as saints, for heaven's sake!

Then there's Judas; the only one who didn't run; the only one who didn't hide; the only one who did his part. Because he didn't run and hide, he is reviled and despised.

It's not fair.

Remove the Threat

"Do you want me to release for you the King of the Jews?" (Pilate) realized that it was out of jealousy that the chief priests had handed (Jesus) over. But the chief priests stirred up the crowd to have him release Barabbas instead. (Mark 15:8-11)

Not long ago, a prominent televangelist made a statement during his broadcast in which he intimated that someone somewhere should most likely be killed as a result of that someone's activities. Though the televangelist later retracted his statement, what does it say that someone, reportedly a person of faith in one who has been called "the Prince of Peace," would advocate the execution/assassination of another human being? I find that troublesome, to say the least. For many people, this televangelist is the closest thing they have to thoughts of a spiritual nature. Can you imagine what might happen if some were to decide that, since this "icon" has advocated the killing of people with whom we don't agree, it must be OK with God if we knock off a few fundamentalist types, or a few Revised Standard Version reading reprobates, or maybe some Buddhists, or a gay person or two? That's downright scary; that's what that is.

On the day Jesus was executed, the very same thing was happening. The chief priests didn't want it to be said that they had Jesus killed, but they wanted him killed nonetheless. So they invented some nonsense about him being a political insurrectionist. Pilate didn't buy it for a minute. But he was in a bind. If he did what was right, he'd have the political and religious leadership (and constituency) in this little, out-of-the-way corner of the empire worked up into a frenzy that would make controlling them impossible. If he did what was expedient, an innocent man would die. So, he gives them a choice. "I'll tell you what," says he. "I'll give you your choice of who goes free and who gets executed. Jesus—the peace loving carpenter, or Barabbas, the militant, murdering participant in the recent rebellion." Now that was a no-brainer; or so Pilate thought. "Why, release Barabbas, of course," came the reply! The thing was Barabbas was no threat to the religious order. In fact, he most likely wasn't much of a temple-going man. Jesus, on the other hand, was seen by the chief priests as direct competition for the attention of the religious faithful. In a free enterprise economic system, competition is a good thing. In the religious game of "God likes me best." it is annoying at best, and deadly at worst. So, the chief priests did what they had to do to remove the competition. This had nothing to do with the religion of which they were a part; this had to do with people in positions of power and authority who felt that their power and authority were being questioned and threatened. So, they removed the threat.

It seems to me that the only people in this world who are truly threatened by the personalities or actions of others are those who have no confidence in their own personalities or abilities to act. That's too bad.

From Scoundrel to Saint

Now when the centurion, who stood facing him, saw that in this way he breathed his last, he said, "Truly this man was a son of God." (Mark 15:39)

Some people have this way of immediately transforming from scoundrel to saint. All they have to do to achieve this remarkable transformation is die. It's that easy.

I know people who have been rejected, derided, abused, and taken for granted and lived sad or angry lives because of their relationship with a rejecting, over-looking abuser. Something happens that brings about the abuser's death and history morphs itself into a different reality. "She was the best woman I ever knew," a son or daughter might say. "What about all those times she told you how worthless and pitiful you are," asks someone who knows the truth. "Don't ever say anything bad about her again," screams the son or daughter. The transformation is complete.

So here we have this soldier. Earlier that morning, he had been one of a group of troops who drew the duty of scourging a prisoner. All part of a normal day's work in an occupied territory when you work for the occupier. Of course, scourging was much more fun than standing guard in the marketplace. At least there was a little activity involved in this process. You got to tie some little pieces of sharp metal into a rope and then rip the hide off a person's back with it. Fun stuff.

After the scourging, the troops trudged up to the top of the city dump following this guy who they had just beaten senseless while he lugged up a four by four cross beam which was strapped across those shoulders they just turned into dog meat. Then came the final part of the day's activity—driving nails through the man's hands to secure him to that cross beam, fastening it to an upright, and hoisting upright, cross beam, and man into the air.

That had been the morning's work for our intrepid centurion. Actually, since all this happened by nine in the morning, he and his buddies had pretty much put in a whole days work already. Still, the last part of the process was the most boring. They had to stand guard to make no one tried to take the man down before he died.

Six hours they stood there. Finally about three in the afternoon, the man on the cross started talking to God. After talking to God for a while, he shouted once and died. As the centurion stood there, waiting to make sure the man was dead before he lowered him back down, he becomes reflective and muses, "You know, he wasn't such a bad guy, really."

No doubt about it; the status of many people rises considerably once they're dead.

You Ain't A'washin' My Feet!

Peter said to (Jesus), "You will never wash my feet." (John 13:8)

It was Maundy Thursday, 1984. I was serving as the Stated Supply Pastor of the Jacoby Chapel United Presbyterian Church in rural Warrensburg, Missouri. I was just a couple of years removed from my seminary indoctrination (in fact, I was still in the employ of the seminary during the week). I was full of idealistic, ivory-tower inspired notions and figured now would be as good a time as any to try something new and improved. I had worked with these folks for two years and we knew each other pretty well, and I figured I wouldn't make anybody too irate. So, on Palm Sunday, I announced that the Maundy Thursday worship would include a foot-washing observance. A few folks squirmed in their pews and Laverne Parsons giggled out loud. I wondered if maybe the only feet I'd have available to wash would be my own.

On Maundy Thursday, I arrived at the church house early and got my pan of water and my drying rag ready. To my complete surprise and utter amazement, nearly the entire congregation came wandering in over the next several minutes. The last person to arrive was Christie Wilson. Christie was in her late 60's, was widowed and took no nonsense from anyone at anytime; most especially not from me. She saw the pan of water sitting there and said, "Preacher, you really intend to carry on with this scheme of yours?" To which I replied as humbly as I could, "Yes, with those for whom it seems a right and appropriate thing to do." Well," she retorted, "You ain't a'washin' my feet, and I got my pantyhose on to make sure you don't! You're my preacher, and it just ain't right." "That's fine," I replied in my best pastoral voice, "You may choose not to participate."

At the point in the proceedings when I began the foot washing, I knelt in front of Don Parsons (Laverne's brother-in-law), wiped his feet with water, dried them off and said, "In the name of God, I am your servant." I proceeded around the room offering the same service to each person there. Along about the fifth or sixth pair of feet, out of the corner of my eye I noticed Christie get up and walk toward the outside door. I figured that she had seen enough and couldn't take anymore. I continued on around the circle of my friends. As I was finishing with the last person, the door opened and Christie came walking back in carrying her pantyhose in her hand. She sat back down and said, "Wash 'em good, Preacher!"

Jesus taught a lot of good lessons while he was at it. What he taught the disciples by washing their feet was that to follow in his footsteps was to willingly accept a life of service to their fellow human beings. To follow in his footsteps means exactly the same thing now as it did then.

The only thing is, most women I know think whoever invented pantyhose ought to be put in the stocks on the courthouse square and subjected to public ridicule and scorn for a day or two.

Most Love is Selfish

"Do you love me? Feed my lambs ... tend my sheep ... feed my sheep." (John 21:15-17)

I get really tired of hearing people talking about how they love hot fudge sundaes, and their new clothes, and somebody else's car, and the smell of chicken frying. In fact, I get really tired of hearing most people talk about love at all. My experience is that most people equate love with something they get or someone they get it from. Love is an emotion. How can it be engendered by ice cream, or clothing, or cars, or even by a smell? If it can be so engendered, then I find the whole notion unusual, strange and odd.

Why can't people say what they mean and be done with it? "I love hot fudge sundaes." Doesn't that really mean, "I find the taste of said confection to be pleasing?" "I love this new dress." Translation: "I think this dress makes me look good." "I love Bob's new sports car." Translation: "I want Bob's new sports car."

Even more insidious is when people say to other people, "I love you." I have no lack of certainty at all that this most often means, "I like how I feel when you're around," or "being seen in your company is really good for my image," or "because of you, I'm not alone," or "you'll do until someone (or something) better comes along." In each case, the emphasis is not on the "you" being loved; the emphasis is on the "I" claiming to love "you." I'm convinced that love is pretty much selfish and self-centered.

Jesus agreed with me, I think. He tried out his theory on Peter. Three times, Peter was asked, "Do you love me?" Three times Peter responded, "Well, of course." Three times, Jesus knew that Peter was thinking about what loving Jesus was doing for him. So, three times, Jesus told Peter (and us, not coincidentally) that if real love is anything, it is selfless. "Feed my lambs, tend my sheep, feed my sheep."

In other words, real love has nothing to do with anything we might receive or anyone from whom we might receive it. It has everything to do with what we can give and to whom we might give it. Real love is a commission. Real love should be who we are and should motivate what we do. For love to be real, it must be focused on somebody else.

"I just love my new underwear." Yeah; right.

Holy Spirit Rush

When the day of Pentecost had come, there were all together in one place. And suddenly from heaven there came a sound like the rush of a violent wind, and it filled the entire house where they were sitting … All of them were filled with the Holy Spirit … (Acts 2:1-2, 4a)

Almost fourteen years ago, Roxanne went into labor three months too early. After three days of doctors trying to keep her from having a baby, she had a baby anyway. At least, we were told it was a baby. When we went to the neonatal intensive care unit, what we were shown lying in the incubator looked far more like a recently-skinned squirrel; a two-pound, nine-ounce skinned squirrel which had just completed its first post-placental defecation. The nurse looked at Roxanne and me and said, "Who's going to clean up that mess? I'm not." Seeing the look of shocked anxiety which came upon Rox's face, I stepped right up and said, "Why not?" As I stuck my hands through the two portals of the incubator and touched, not a skinned squirrel, but our daughter, Cristina, for the first time, the top of my head started tingling and the tingling feeling quickly spread all the way to my toes. I had always called experiences like that the "chill bumps." My friend, Bobb, insists that it is what he calls a "Holy Spirit Rush." I do know that it was a holy moment for me.

Fast forward almost fourteen years. The other night, that little two-pound, nine-ounce miracle walked across a stage at our local high school and received a diploma signifying her graduation from junior high school. As I watched her walk across that stage, the top of my head started tingling and the tingling feeling quickly spread all the way to my toes. It was another holy moment; it was another "Holy Spirit Rush."

I really don't care that there is a perfectly rational, physiological explanation for the above-mentioned sensation. I only experience it during holy moments. It only happens when I am being rushed by God's spirit.

If At First You Don't Succeed

"This Jesus is the stone that was rejected by you, the builders; it has become the cornerstone." (Acts 4:11)

I've been told that Michael Jordan was cut from his high school basketball team. Albert Einstein failed high school mathematics. Thomas Edison tried a thousand times before he came up with a light bulb that suited him. I once got a C+ on a urine test. What do all these famous personages have in common?

Michael Jordan became a better than average basketball player. Albert Einstein finally figured out that all things are relative. Thomas Edison eventually came up with a way to shine light on the world. I now routinely get B's on my urine tests. Despite early questionable performances and poor evaluations, each of these guys went on to do remarkable things which left indelible marks on the world. Nondescript beginnings; history-making results.

Peter and John are on the way up to the Jerusalem church house for prayer meeting. Just before they get there, they have the opportunity to help out a guy who is having a problem with ambulation. This, of course, does not go unnoticed. Peter takes the opportunity to get in a little oratory practice. He summons the gawkers who have congregated to gather around, and tells them a story. He harkens back a few years. "Remember when Jesus was here trying to tell you that there just might be a better way to have a relationship with God than what y'all had been doing? You weren't in much of a mood to listen. In fact you stood by and watched the man die. Well, guess what? He lives on in John and in me and in many others who were able to catch a glimpse of what he was saying to us. Because he lives on in us, we seek to offer aid whenever we can, just as he did. Because he lives in us, we were able to offer our new friend a hand with his problem." The more Peter talked, the more people listened. By the time the choir got around to singing "Just As I Am," Luke says that about 5,000 folks went forward and signed pledge cards.

The stone that the builders rejected became the cornerstone. The kid from Nazareth stood the world on its ear just by telling people to get along; really get along. That was threatening for religious muckety-mucks whose very existence was built upon separating themselves from those who didn't meet their standards.

I wonder what would happen if Peter and John could go on another speaking tour and stand on the steps of the capitols of a few countries and tell the story again. The world just might get stood on its ear again.

I Ain't Mad

"… I was so enraged with them, I pursued them even to foreign cities." (Acts 26:11)

I believe anger is a lie. When we express ourselves through anger, we are being dishonest. A whole lot of aggravation could be spared if people could just be honest with one another about what they are feeling in the first place. I've heard it said that the thing about lying is that once you do it the first time, you find yourself doing it again to justify the first lie and on and on. It's the same with anger. I think it's just more bother than it's worth.

So says Paul as he makes his defense before King Agrippa. He is recounting once again what has transpired in his life to bring him to where he now stands. "Them" are the followers of Jesus who Paul (Saul at the time) was pledged to destroy.

I think it's interesting that he uses the word "enraged" to describe his emotional state at the time. This interests me because I have come up with a theory/observation/opinion after working with human beings for so many years. My spouse, the clinical psychotherapist has even said that she agrees with me … to a point. I believe that rage/anger is not a base emotion. I can honestly say that in 54 years of being alive, I have never once seen anger displayed when anger was what the person was honestly feeling. My experience of anger is that it is always a "smoke screen" emotion for things like fear, or jealousy, or inadequacy, or disappointment, or … I could go on and on. To openly express any of these emotions is to open oneself completely to what may seem like unfathomable risk. After all, these are emotions that denote weakness. If it becomes known that something or someone is feared, then that something or someone wields control. Jealousy will push others away quicker than anything I know. Inadequacy and disappointment prevent us from doing or being whatever it is God would have us do or be. Anger or rage, on the other hand, is a powerful, strong emotion. It gives us a feeling of being in control. It creates the feeling that others can be made to feel all those weak emotions that the angry person will not or cannot accept or admit.

It's just that people who get angry really make me mad.

Let's Get Along

"… so far as it depends on you, live peaceably with all." (Romans 12:18)

Lately the print, broadcast, and online media have found newsworthy the most interesting phenomenon. I can't say that it is a new phenomenon, but I can say that it had never entered the vast, cavernous emptiness that is my mind. The phenomenon of which I speak, of course, is the funeral protest. Yes, friends, the funeral protest. For reasons that only those conducting said protests understand, that sensitive time of grief and mourning that folks use to mark the death of a loved one is now a time to voice inappropriate, albeit heart-felt, social or religious convictions. Specifically, there is a group of folks representing a small, Midwestern church which is traveling about boisterously disrupting memorials to persons who have given their lives in the current conflicts in which the United States is militarily involved. If the protesters were stating their opposition to the conflict, based on their faith convictions, that might be understandable, if still unacceptable. These folks are making their way to funerals to make the point that the dead person is dead as God's punishment for perceived evils which our society sanctions. If that doesn't make any sense to you, it shouldn't. It doesn't make any sense to me. Not only that, but these folks have a lawyer and say they will sue anybody who tries to get them to desist from their disruptive behavior.

The whole thing defies any attempt at rational explanation I try to apply to it. These are people who claim to be disciples of Jesus. These are people who claim to be in the apostolic succession which included such noteworthy folks as Peter, Paul and Mary (Magdalene). And yet, because of a distorted view of "God's will" they are using God's name to validate a message of wrath and hatred. What happened to the message of peace? What happened to the message of unity? How can these sisters and brothers claim that something angers God for no better reason than they don't like whatever that something happens to be? What does their message say to all those people who are trying to come to grips with the reality of God in the first place?

All I know is this, "… so far as it depends on (me), I want to live peaceably with all."

Feeling Alright

"... Blessed be God ... who consoles us in all our affliction, so that we may able to console those who are in any affliction ..." (II Corinthians 1:3-4)

Physically speaking, I've been a mess for a while. Three years ago after two surgeries to fuse my cervical vertebrae together, I was hurting so much all of the time that my employer put me on permanent disability. I haven't worked full-time sense then. In the fall of 2004, my family doctor made an appointment for me to see a neurological specialist at the Cleveland Clinic in Ohio. That doctor indicated that I had a neurological disease that was irreversible and had a 100 percent mortality rate. To say that my affliction got the better of me would be an understatement. For about six months, I tried to put up with that as best I could. Then, in the spring of 2005, a neurologist I was visiting with closer to home asked if I would be willing to submit to a couple of more tests. I agreed, and the results of the tests were that the doctor in Ohio was wrong and that I don't have the disease he led me to believe I have. After finally making connections with the right kind of doctor (a rheumatologist) I was, at long last properly diagnosed as having fibromyalgia. Now, there's no cure for that either, but I'll die when I'm supposed to instead of when a disease decides I should.

I thought about feeling sorry for myself for a while, and there are days when I get tired of hurting. But, as an old friend of mine likes to say, "I'm upright and breathing." I have gained a whole new appreciation for people who live for many years with some ailment, or infirmity, or affliction.

That's the very thing that Paul is referring to in his opening lines of what has come to be known as II Corinthians. He had put up with an ailment of his own, and now he thanks God for comforting him. Paul apparently didn't have the notion that God had healed him of anything, but instead was thankful God was with him and eased the suffering a little bit.

Then, Paul makes a pretty profound leap in his thinking. First he thanks God for hanging in there with him while he was hurting. Then he says that because he had the experience of God suffering with him, now he is able to suffer with others. It almost sounds like Paul figures living with the "affliction" was a good thing and that it made him an even better ambassador for God in the lives of people.

Thinking about that makes me feel kind of foolish because I'm a big baby, and I whine when I hurt. I think maybe I ought to redirect a little of that self-pity and use the energy it takes for something more constructive, like learning to play the banjo.

But, Doing the Right Thing is Hard!

"... let us not grow weary of doing what is right ..." (Galatians 6:9)

When I was 52 years old, I came to the realization of someone else I want to be when I grow up. I realized that I wanted to be a school teacher. I had spent the past year doing some substitute teaching in our local school district, and had some fun in the process. Mostly, I taught in classrooms where the students were receiving specialized services because they had been classified as having some sort of a learning exceptionality. I had so much fun, that I went back to school myself (something I swore I'd never do!), so I could find out a few things about sharing knowledge with these special students.

As I write this note, I'm doing what is called student teaching. That means that I'm getting in some practice before I actually walk into an elementary or secondary classroom as the instructor of record. It feels kind of strange since I've been teaching for 42 years already. It all started when the junior high Sunday School teacher didn't show up and I covered for him at the tender age of 12. There's another story for another time if ever there was one.

Today another teacher came to me with a look of resigned frustration in her eyes. She explained that for two weeks she's been trying to help a student with whom she works to say the word "has," and asked me if I would give it a try. The student could, without difficulty, produce the sound that each individual letter makes. However, when asked to put those three sounds together, he consistently pronounced a new and entirely original word. My colleague grabbed hold of her hair and said, "What else can I do?" She knows that the right thing is to continue working with our young friend. Right now, though she is tired of trying.

Paul knew the feeling all too well. In trying to do what he perceived to be the "right thing" he had been laughed at, spit on, ran out of town, beaten to a pulp, and had contracted a few different maladies. Even so, in this letter he writes to the cantankerous, contentious folks in the churches up in Galatia, he can say, "Let us not grow weary of doing what is right."

Every person with a conscience knows that doing the right thing is the right thing to do. This maxim holds true no matter how tired, or frustrated, or weary, or exasperated we get.

Do You Believe in Angels?

"(The Son) has become as much superior to angels as the name he has inherited is more excellent than theirs ... Are not all angels spirits in the divine service, sent to serve for the sake of those who are to inherit salvation?" (Hebrews 1:4, 14)

Once upon a time, in a lifetime far, far away, a preaching teacher said that any homiletical discourse which relies on prooftexting to substantiate its major points is suspect at best, and most likely irrelevant. Translated into American, that means if a person feels need to lift a biblical statement from its context here and another from over there, then that person ought to abandon the enterprise. The most inappropriate and biblically dishonest thing a person can do is use a few words that says something he or she wants to say without disregard for what comes before or after.

I make my statement about prooftexting because, in the verses that stand between the two which I have lifted from their context above, the author of Hebrews has gratuitously lifted several statements from their context in order to make his or her point concerning Jesus. This is done for a reason which I find bewildering if not amusing. The author wants to establish that Jesus holds a higher rank in the heavenly pecking order than do angels. Of course, to the people of the time, reality was ascribed to angels as surely as it was to demons. In fact, at one point in the book, humankind is described as being just a little less than angels in that pecking order (Psalm 8:5). Thus, to say that Jesus has passed the angels in superiority is like saying Tony Stewart slipped past Jeff Gordon coming out of the fourth corner at Talladega to win the race. It turns what is known to be real upside down. It also drives the wedge a little deeper between the upstart Jesus followers and their spiritual ancestors. To make sure that there is no mistake about the point being made, the author of Hebrews uses several verses taken, as I said before, out of their context in the Hebrew scripture to prove his point.

Maybe you believe in angels; maybe you don't. I suppose that might depend on how deep and wide you are willing to make your reality. I can't say one way or another whether I believe in angels. I've never met one so far as I know.

I could, however, tell you about a few fine, upstanding unicorns I've had the pleasure of meeting.

Holy Ed?

"Like obedient children, do not be conformed to the desires that you formerly had in ignorance. Instead, as he who called you is holy, be holy yourselves in all your conduct." (I Peter 1:14-16)

This is an interestingly cryptic little morsel within an interestingly cryptic little epistle. The people who study this stuff for a living have pretty much concluded that this is another piece of literature written by someone unknown to the ages who used the name of someone very well known to the ages so that the letter would get a widespread reading. In other words, Peter didn't write this. It's still fun to figure out what it's about.

The letter is addressed to several enclaves of believers spread throughout part of Asia Minor at a time when believers pretty much all had a bounty on their heads because, for some unknown reason, they just couldn't bring themselves to recognize Caesar as being a god on an equal plain with the great God Almighty, Maker of Heaven and Earth. It is these folks who are compared to children, albeit obedient children, by our intrepid author. I suppose it might be an analogy of some merit. Any of us who have been children at one time or another in our lives may well recall being taught the advantages of being obedient. We may further recall having pointed out to us the utter folly of desires we may or may not have harbored as a result of our immature ignorance. For example, how was I to know that it was not considered good form to take off my shoes, go to the back of the room, get a running start and see how far I could slide on those wonderfully slick old wood floors in the Landessville Grade School when I was but a wee lad of six years old? I learned the folly of my lack of form when, in the midst of the most perfect slide of my life, Mrs. Wine re-entered the room and my slide ended at her feet because she had chosen to block the end of the runway.

Despite the fact that we have all formerly succumbed to desires, such as my desire to set the all-time record for longest slide on a newly waxed wood floor, which ultimately proved to reveal our ignorance, we are called to be "holy." How in the world can an old, unrepentant floor slider such as me achieve the status of holy? I'm not sure I even want to be holy; I can't even begin to imagine what might be contained in the job description.

I think what the author is saying to his readers is this: Given that the powers that be take great pleasure in torturing and killing people for no better reason than their allegiance to Jesus, being on our best behavior at all times and in all places would be considered a show of some considerable wisdom. In other words, give those who would condemn you no reason to do so.

That is still good advice. There are those who are diligent in trying to catch people of faith stumbling or even falling. "See, I told you they aren't perfect," is their mantra. So; be holy.

Hmm ... I've heard of holy mackerel, and holy cow, and even holey old blue jeans, but holy Ed? I must admit, that will take a bit of getting used to.

You'll Grow Into It

"Rid yourselves of all malice and guile, insincerity, envy, and all slander.
Like newborn infants ... you may grow into salvation." (I Peter 2:1-2)

My birthday is coming up in a couple of days. I'll be 54 years young; it seems like just today I was only 53. Even though I can't remember my own name most of the time, I can remember my birthday 45 years ago with great clarity. If my subtraction is correct, that would have been my ninth birthday. That day I got my first bicycle. It was a beauty, let me tell you! It was a bright red J.C. Higgins from Sears, Roebuck, and Company. It had a headlight on the front and a luggage rack on the back. I knew that I would be stylin' on that bike. There was only one detail that dampened my joy and enthusiasm just ever so slightly. It was a 26-inch bright red J.C. Higgins bicycle. I was something of a sickly child up until I was eight years old, and as I celebrated my ninth birthday, I had not yet put all vestiges of runtdom behind me. That is by way of saying that the bicycle was quite tall from my vantage point. Looking straight at it from the front, the handle bars were at eye level. When I pointed out this anomaly to my loving parents, Dad sagely commented, "You'll grow into it." He was right. On my 17th birthday, I successfully mounted that bicycle without benefit of the top back porch step for the first time.

All of that is to introduce a comment or two I have about the blasphemous heresy the author of this letter that bears Peter's name utters here in the second chapter. "Like newborn infants ... you may grow into salvation." Why, somebody should have stoned him on the spot. Everybody knows that you don't grow into salvation. Depending on your point of view, you either go with Brother Brown down to Piney Creek and get dunked and are thereby saved, or you start speaking French when your native language is German and are thereby saved, or some guy with a name like the Right Reverend Doctor Jimmy Joe Johnson (sporting his greasy, slicked back hair and powder blue polyester leisure suit with white plastic belt and matching white plastic shoes) scares the living hell out of you in a tent somewhere on a sultry July night and you are thereby saved. So, what's with this business of growing into salvation?

I remember when a bishop put his hands on top of my newly permed hair and asked me if I was "going on to perfection" as he presumed to do something God had already done (that would be ordaining me). I figured that meant about the same thing as growing into salvation which, as I already mentioned, is blasphemous heresy. I started to rise up so that I could point out to the bishop the heretical nature of his question when the fingers on the end of a hand belonging to somebody else wrapped themselves into the curls of my newly permed hair and gave them a lusty jerk. It turns out that those fingers were on the end of my lovely wife's right hand.

The reality is that salvation is something everyone grows into, despite protests to the contrary. Not only that, the process never ends. The author of this letter was right on the money. The best advice is to keep your nose and various other appendages clean as you seek to be the best person of faith you can be. The minute somebody figures they are "saved," the trouble (and the fun) begins.

"Please" and "Thank You"

"Do not repay evil for evil or abuse for abuse; but, on the contrary, repay with a blessing." (I Peter 3:9)

Sometimes I have the opportunity to work with young people who are considered to have a severe behavior problem. Many of them draw all their energy and strength from their desire for revenge. Holding people personally responsible for slights, either real or perceived, is what they get out of bed for in the morning. Suggest to them that they offer who ever has offended them some sort of blessing and the response will most likely be uproarious laughter. One of these students played a major role in a large city gang before moving to our small community recently. His life so far has taught him that everybody is out to get him. Every time I see him do something good, or positive, or helpful, I make a point of saying "Thank You" and telling him how much his efforts are appreciated. More often than not he responds with a simple nod or sometimes a verbal "You're Welcome." It is such a simple little blessing that I offer him, but he responds appropriately nonetheless.

How many times have you heard some person, in an attempt to justify a vengeful attitude, say, "The Bible says an eye for an eye and a tooth for a tooth"? I have heard it far more times than I care to recollect. In the original Jewish sacred text, it does say this in response to specific circumstances under certain conditions at a precise time in history. Even so, people look past all of the wonderful language about nonretaliation and conciliation also contained in both the Jewish and Christian writings. Revenge is a powerful motivator for many people. It drives those people to do mean-spirited or even deadly things in an attempt to exact "justice."

With that backdrop, the author of I Peter gives instruction that might sound completely ludicrous if it weren't so God-like. "Do not repay evil for evil or abuse for abuse; but, on the contrary, repay with a blessing." Repay with a blessing! Sounds hopelessly naïve, don't you think? It is in our nature to want to get even. We want to give as good as we get. Somebody has to pay!

The world would be an incredible place if leaders of governments could start looking for the positive. It would be fun to watch what would happen if the main tools of international diplomacy were "Please" and "Thank You."

MAY I ASK WHO IS CALLING?

On Losing the Lottery

One of the men who have accompanied us during all the time that Jesus went in and out among us ... must become a witness with us ... They cast lots for them, and the lot fell on Matthias, and he was added to the eleven disciples. (Acts 1:21-22, 26)

Reese and I went to southern Missouri one February to do some winter fishing. Along the way, we made a fuel and rest stop at a little convenience store in a town I know longer remember. When I came out of the bathroom, Reese handed me a lottery ticket. It was one of those "scratch and sniff" things. Now, Reese was a member of the church council and so he knew the dim view the religious hierarchy took of gambling in any form. I tried to give the thing back, but he said, "We're not in Iowa. If you win, I'll claim it and split the proceeds with you."

The jackpot for this particular game of chance was $165,000. To win, there had to be four matching pictures out of six on the card. I scratched off picture number one: a horse. I scratched off picture number two: a horse. I got really nervous as I scratched off picture number three: a cow. With an audible sigh of relief, I scratched off picture number four: a chicken. With less trepidation, I scratched off picture number five: another horse! I was scared to death as I very tentatively scratched off the sixth and final picture: a duck. "Thank God," I thought, "I didn't win!"

Luke gives us the impression that there had been quite a number of people who had become "disciples" of Jesus along the way, and had traveled many roads with him. When Peter finally said that having 11 members of the inner circle was not good form, they looked around at the folks gathered, and decided for what ever reason that two of them were worthy of consideration to become the new 12th man. There was a man named Joseph Barsabbas and another guy named Matthias. The 11 talked it over for a while and couldn't make a decision. Finally, they did something that would make a lot of good and faithful Christian folks cringe. They gambled; that's right, they played a game of chance. Luke says that they "cast lots." In other words, they flipped a coin. Matthias called "heads," it came up heads, and he was elected to receive the 12th spot.

I'm going to go buy a lottery ticket and I'm not going to feel a bit guilty.

Thou Shalt Not Be Different

(The Sadducees) called them and ordered them not to speak or teach at all in the name of Jesus. But Peter and John answered them, "Whether it is right in God's sight to listen to you rather than to God, you must judge; for we cannot keep from speaking about what we have seen and heard." (Acts 4:18-20)

Bobb walked back to the dormitory at the seminary and I could see from his countenance that something was bothering him. That I could see this was extraordinary because Bobb is one of the most emotionally level people I will ever know. I waited for a few minutes and then cautiously approached the door to his room. "Are you O.K?" was my introductory inquiry. "Why can't they let me be me?" was his response. Not long before that time, Bobb had an experience in which he felt led by God to speak in a language other than his own. Now, I don't understand that sort of thing at all. Nonetheless, the experience had a very profound effect on Bobb. In some ways, it was a type of defining experience for him. On this day, seminary professors had confronted and challenged Bobb because of his convictions regarding his foray into the world of glossalalia. He felt threatened and attacked and devalued.

I held Bobb while he wept and comforted him as best I could. After a while, speaking brother to brother, I said something like, "Whether it is right in God's sight for you to listen to the professors rather than God, you'll have to judge. But, I really don't think you should stop speaking about what you have seen and heard," or words to that effect.

Then there was the time my friend, Charlie, was berated by a bunch of theological holier-than-thous because he asserted that he could see God in all of nature. This, of course, is a blasphemous heresy called pantheism. It is also a blasphemous heresy which I share with Charlie.

I, for one, will judge no person's convictions if they are heart-felt and are intended for the good of others and do no harm to anyone.

I'm Too Nice

"Lord, grant to Your servants to speak Your word with all boldness, while You stretch out Your hand to heal, and signs and wonders are performed ... When they had prayed, they were all filled with the Holy Spirit and spoke the word of God with boldness." (Acts 4:29-31)

I wish I were more like those early disciples. Sitting in the safety of my office typing away, I can be pretty bold. I tend, though, to wilt a bit when given the opportunity to share my convictions in a public forum. Instead of telling the truth as I understand it, I seek ways to say things in such a way as not to offend. Often, my point never gets made because I have buried it in polite correctness. I wonder if I am disappointing God when I feel the call to be a prophet but compromise the prophet's message so that people will still like me.

A guy named Wesley once said that, in his opinion, faith should be informed by four things: scripture, reason, tradition and experience. The Sadducees Luke writes about in the book of Acts were big on scripture (their interpretation), reason (what made sense to them), and tradition (tradition was *very* important to them). Experience, though, was a different matter. Who could say if an experience was valid or not?

Peter and John had just returned from their interview with the Sadducees. They had shared with the other members of the community (apparently now numbering about 5,000) that they had been ordered not to do anything else in Jesus' name. In other words, they were to stick to scripture, reason and tradition. Their experience was controversial, heretical, and upsetting to the status quo.

Interestingly, when the rest of the community heard this, instead of saying, "Well, alrighty, then," they had an impromptu prayer meeting during which they asked God to make them bold enough to talk about their experiences even more. As far as they were concerned, they were right and it would have been wrong for them not to say so.

Dad has told me more than once that I'm "too damned nice a guy." He's right.

Don't We Know You?

When (Saul) reached Jerusalem, he tried to join the body of disciples there; but they were afraid of him, because they did not believe that he was really a convert. (Acts 9:26)

What is it somebody said about not teaching an old dog new tricks? Pretty often, that holds true. However, it is not always the case. Even when it's not the case, anybody who knows the dog is not going to be very quick to believe that anything has changed. They'll still insist that the poor old pooch be kept on a short leash.

Everybody living in the countries on the east end of the Mediterranean knew who Saul was. He had built himself up quite a reputation that was either good or bad, depending on whom you asked. Then, one day he walked into Jerusalem and started telling anybody who would listen that Jesus was the Messiah, the Son of God; the Savior of the world. I can imagine what the followers of Jesus were saying to one another. "Can you believe this guy? Who is he trying to fool? I'll bet he's just trying to lure us out in the open." I wouldn't have believed it, would you?

I'm not going to lie, after my Dad's "blinding light" experience, I wasn't sure what to believe. Don't get me wrong, he wasn't a bad sort before, but church stuff wasn't part of what he did. It took living with him for a while and seeing that his priorities had changed to convince me.

So, here we have old Saul, Judaism's self-proclaimed exterminator of those who followed Jesus, walking into the very center of the Jewish world and saying, "Guess what, I was wrong; Jesus was right." People didn't know what to believe.

Sometimes the new path we're given to travel as disciples is difficult to negotiate at first because of the path we were walking down before. We should not be deterred. God knows the truth and people with their eyes open and their mouths shut will see the truth. As turned out to be the case with Saul and my dad, often the people who some see as least likely wind up being a model that others look up to.

What Is She Doing Here?

"This is the man who is teaching everyone against our people, our law, and this place; more than that, he has actually brought Greeks into the temple and has defiled this holy place." (Acts 21:28)

"What is *she* doing here?" That was the question murmured none too quietly one morning just before worship was to begin in a small town church where I was serving as the pastor. *She* was a gracious woman of deep faith who was visiting a former co-worker who attended the church. *She* was also of a different racial and ethnic heritage than any who worshipped regularly at the church. "What is *she* doing here?"

Along comes Saul (now Paul), the former Christian killer, who is quickly becoming a quite proficient teller of the Jesus story. The problem is Paul is so excited about the story that he doesn't much care who he tells. He's just as likely to tell a Greek or a Roman about Jesus as he is to share with good and faithful Jews. Paul wants everybody to know.

In fact, he has built such a reputation for sharing the story with people who are Gentiles, that he even gets accused of it when he hasn't done it. Such is the case in Acts 21. Some dyed-in-the-wool folks claim that he had the audacity to take a Greek into the temple. Whether this actually happened or not, they think it did, and that is enough to get them riled up. The thing is, this is another instance of something other than God being worshipped. "He has defiled this holy place," was the accusation. Some of them probably were asking one another, "What's *he* doing here?"

I don't understand how it is that 2000 years later, in a place dedicated to worshipping God in the name of Jesus where the stories about him and Paul and others are told with great affection, it is still possible that a professed disciple can wonder out loud, "What is *she* doing here?" I'm not being judgmental; just curious.

There's some backward thinking going on. People apparently have the notion that God belongs to them and that they can control who has access to God and who does not.

God must surely be laughing uproariously at the silliness of it all. Or, maybe God's looking skeptically at all of us and wondering, "What are *they* doing here?"

It's something to think about.

Who Did I Say I Am?

The tribune came and asked Paul, "Tell me, are you a Roman citizen?" And (Paul) said, "Yes." ... *(Paul) called out in the council, "Brothers, I am a Pharisee, a son of Pharisees." (Acts 22:27; 23:6)*

Did you ever give thought to all of the different people you are? For example, depending on who you talk to, I am a father, a husband, a son, a brother, a nephew, a cousin, a pastor, a teacher, a musician, and/or a counselor. There are some days when a couple of those people that I am run into each other because they are going in different directions. There are other days when two or three of those people come together in response to some situation in which I find myself. The father/teacher/counselor trifecta is one I pull off successfully from time to time.

Paul is running into all kinds of problems in Jerusalem. The Jews are mad at him for talking like a crazy man about this Jesus business. The Romans aren't very happy with him because it looks to them like he is disturbing the peace. Paul finds out that there is a time when being different people comes in handy. First the Romans decide to give him a whooping so that hopefully the maddening crowd outside will de-madden a little. Paul pulls out his first ace in the hole. "Guess what, old buddies," he informs them just as the beating is about to commence, "I'm one of you; I'm a Roman citizen." Oops! Those soldiers back off in a hurry once they are informed of that juicy tidbit of information. The next day he goes to a meeting of the ministerial association. Paul starts off the proceedings by saying simply that, up until that point, he had done what he thought God wanted him to do and had a clear conscience about it. For whatever reason, that prompts the president of the association to tell somebody to smack old Paul in the face. Then appears ace in the hole number two. "You want to know something?" Paul asks, "I'm a Pharisee, and my daddy was a Pharisee, too."

Throughout the remainder of his life, Paul maintained these two credentials; Roman citizen and Pharisee, and pulled them out often in order to further the cause in situations which required that he do so.

I'm rather of the notion that we are all given the responsibility of being several people because it gives us the chance to communicate with a whole lot of folks. It gets a little exhausting trying to keep up, but all in all our multiple selves are a gift.

I just wish I could remember who I'm supposed to be when.

Many Are Called

"Every high priest chosen from among mortals is put in charge of things per-taining to God. And one does not presume to take this honor, but takes it only when called by God." (Hebrews 5:1, 4)

When I was a young boy, I would hope that I would get a call to go to some-where up the road to play baseball. When I did get a call and made my way wher-ever the game was to be played, then I hoped that I wouldn't be the last one chosen. I wasn't a very good baseball player, and so I got all kinds of excited when I got the call to play. I had been called and I had been chosen.

Fast forward about 25 years. I had begun my seminary indoctrination and was getting acquainted with others who had embarked on this same journey of theo-logical frivolity. In some class or another, students were asked to describe their "call." One received his call when he heard he could make more money as a preacher than he could stocking shelves at the grocery store. Another said that he received his call when he realized that all he had to do was teach Sunday School and talk for 20 minutes on Sunday morning. Yet another said that she got her call when she realized that there weren't enough women going to seminary and it was up to her to do something about that. There were still others who talked about how antiquated they viewed the concept of receiving a call as being. They chose to work as a professional for the church because, unless they faltered badly, they would always have a job.

Then there was this guy from Indiana by way of Texas, Mississippi, Illinois, Kansas, and Ohio. He said that he wasn't quite sure about being called. What he had been able to figure out was that whenever he tried to pursue what seemed like a decent, livable career, something happened that steered him down another path. For him, it was not so much that he was called as that other options kept falling away for one reason or another.

It stayed that way for twelve more years until that guy finally got his call directly from the source. When it happened, it became even more evident that it was not so much being blinded by heavenly light while ten thousand angels sang the chorus of "Jingle Bells." Rather, it was a sensation akin to having a size 13 steel-toed boot repeatedly applied to the area in and around his gluteus maximus. The amazing thing is that in all the years since then, nothing has changed. The call continues to come on a regular basis in the form of another well-placed, swift kick from that most accurate and swift of kickers; God.

So, people can talk all they want to about their high and holy experience of revelatory light during which they were handed the scrolls of heaven. For a lot of folks like my friend (who, by the way, looks back at me every time I look in a mirror) the call comes in the form of a swift kick. This is far less touchy-feely, and therefore far more effective.

Baa!!

"I exhort the elders among you to tend the flock of God that is in your charge ... be examples to the flock." (I Peter 5:1-3)

I was around a lot of sheep as a young boy because my Grandpa Thomas had some on his little farm. I hope not very many sheep are reading this because I must be honest and say that sheep are some of God's dumber creatures. They are nearly blind, and seem to be totally incapable of independent decision making. They stay in a flock all the time because it just doesn't occur to them not to. If instinct pushes one of them in a certain direction the rest will go that direction, too. Why? Just because; that's why.

Then the author of this letter infers that the old-timers in the communities to which the letter is addressed need to figure out how to be good shepherds. There just has to be some sort of irony here because shepherding was no one's first career of choice. To be a shepherd was among the lowliest of jobs. Most people would do almost anything else rather than resort to shepherding. The best a shepherd could hope for was to maybe be given a few lamb chops as a Hanukkah gift.

It is to these lofty stations that believers and faith community leaders are encouraged to aspire. "All you people in the pews, how well can you say, 'Baa?'" "The rest of you standing up front reading the Torah from the scrolls, get yourselves some border collies and keep the flock together."

Not only that, shepherds are also supposed to show the sheep how to be sheep. "Be examples to the flock," our author says. Watching sheep is one thing; being a sheep is a bit of a stretch.

I guess maybe all those biblical authors thought of sheep when they thought of believers because sheep are basically helpless and are at the mercy of their environment. In many ways, the early believers were in a similar state of affairs. Their lives were constantly at risk. Somebody somewhere thought they were a nuisance and wanted to get rid of them. So, maybe they did need a shepherd to keep them out of trouble.

Thinking of it that way, I would have to agree that those folks who have a little experience at this life of faith business need to be willing to share that experience with those who do not. It won't hurt, and it certainly could help.

Now, I need to go work on my "Baa."

Would You Be Available?

"We have been given us everything needed for life and godliness, through the knowledge of God who called us by God's own glory and goodness." (II Peter 1:3)

Yesterday, I was going about the routine of my day, absorbed in thoughts of little relevance or importance. Then, the telephone rang. To be perfectly honest, the telephone at our house rings an average of 10,438 times per day. In fact, it rings so often that, if I'm absorbed in thoughts of little relevance or importance, I may not even answer it. Instead, there is an electronic version of me who lives in a little box on the nightstand in the bedroom and who never complains about answering for me. Yesterday, though, as I mentioned, my thoughts were basically inconsequential and I was alone in the house so I decided to do something novel and answered the call.

After I gave my perfunctory "Hello, this is Ed Sinclair, how may I be of assistance to you?" I heard a woman's voice that I did not recognize. She identified herself as representing a talent agency in a large city near where I live. The woman went on to say that she had been given my name and number by someone (I already don't remember who) and that she had heard a recording of my musical stylings. "Are you available the last Saturday in May?" she inquired. "Yes," came my tentative reply. "Oh, good!" she exclaimed. "As you may know," she went on, "we have a large music and art festival here attended by tens of thousands of people, and I would love to have you play. You would receive $400 for your performance."

I didn't know what to say. First of all, for the past year or so, when I've gotten out an instrument to play, it has been for my own amusement. Second of all, I've never been called by a talent agent in my life. With my mind desperately trying to shift in to relevant/important mode, I mumbled something about being honored and that I would love to be a part of the festival.

As soon as the conversation ended, I began to worry a bit. What tunes that I've been playing are "road ready?" How much practicing will I need to do? And then, I opened up the book and what did my wondering eyes behold? "We have been given us everything needed for life and godliness, through the knowledge of God who called us by God's own glory and goodness." In the excitement of the moment, I lost track of the fact that I do nothing in a vacuum. The God I like to spend time with has given me talent and ability. I wouldn't have received the call in the first place had this not been so.

When we get a call offering us an opportunity to be of service, be it from God or from a talent agent in a large city nearby, we can be confident that God either has already given us what we need, or that God will give us what we need when the time comes.

In a Blaze of Glory

"What sort of persons ought you to be in leading lives of holiness and godliness, waiting for and hastening the coming of the day of God, because of which the heavens will be set ablaze and dissolved, and the elements will melt with fire?" (II Peter 3:11)

This sounds like the basic plot line for one of those made-for-TV disaster films, doesn't it? Let's see; of course, Charlton Heston will portray God, the rest of humankind will portray themselves, as will the heavens and the elements. That would just tear up the May sweeps ratings, wouldn't it?

On the other hand, scientists who have nothing better to do than figure out things no one needs to know have determined that the sun will die in precisely 5 billion years and our galaxy will go out in a blaze of glory. I don't suppose that the person who wrote these letters and ascribed Peter's name to them had figured out the time table for this grandest of fireworks displays; nonetheless, it is comforting to know that the "day of the Lord" is still 5 billion years off. I plan on being an old man with nothing left to accomplish other than a little fishing and a little guitar playing by that time.

The really important thing that the author ponders is set forth in these words: "What sort of persons ought you to be in leading lives of holiness and godliness?" It is significant that the question is not, "What ought you to be doing?" Far too many people have the entirely misguided notion that holiness and godliness are things to be done in order to secure God's favor and in order to create a template of religious action to which they can then attempt to hold others; damning them when they fail to fit the pattern. Holiness and godliness are not actions to be completed; they are states of being. According to the Sinclair's Completely Subjective and Biased Dictionary of Words I Like to Use from Time to Time, holiness is the sincere and honest attempt by persons to make the spiritual aspect of their nature the primary aspect of their nature. Trust me when I tell you that bibles aren't holy, churches and/or denominations aren't holy, not even cows are holy. Holy are they who recognize that true reality exists on a plane unrecognizable by and unaffected by the three-dimensional plane in which they carry out their day-to-day lives. According to that same dictionary, godliness is exactly what it implies—being like God. Now, don't go thinking I'm all weird and crazy. Only God is God is God is God; I already told you that. Godliness is the attempt to be as much like what we perceive God to be as our human form will allow. The classic orthodox language speaks of the "indwelling of the holy spirit." My understanding of things doesn't get that flowery or awe-inspiring. I do have a notion, though, that the thing that sets homo sapiens apart from the rest of creation is awareness of our truest nature as spiritual beings first and foremost and that it is a bit of godlikeness with which each human being is endowed that makes that awareness possible.

WALKING THE WALK

First-Born

The Lord said to Moses, "Consecrate to me all the firstborn; whatever is the first to open the womb among the Israelites, of human beings and animals, is mine." Moses said to the people, "I sacrifice to the Lord every male that first opens the womb, but every firstborn of my sons I redeem." (Exodus 13:1-3, 15)

I am a firstborn child. Not only that, I'm a firstborn son. In fact, I'm an only born son. After me, Mother and Dad gave up on the son thing and had three daughters instead. There is a lot that can be said about being a firstborn. On the one hand, firstborn children are the ones upon whom the parents experiment as they attempt to learn something about raising children. This can be good or bad depending upon the quality of the experiment and the conditions in which it is conducted. On the other hand, when and if the second born and the third born and how ever many more borns there are come along, being the firstborn becomes a position of honor. It is the firstborn to whom the latter born look for advice and guidance when trying to learn the intricacies of parent manipulation and also how to best avoid detection when being a child takes them outside the parameters of parental acceptance.

As I've been thinking about the story of the Exodus and, specifically, the significance that being firstborn plays in the story, I have found myself wondering with some fascination whose firstborn I would have been had I been born at the time of the Exodus and the decades thereafter. I would like to think I would have been the firstborn of a nice Jewish couple who obediently painted the door with lamb's blood to save my life.

If I read this 13th chapter of Exodus correctly, it might not have been very advantageous to have been born to the nice Jewish couple in the years following the Exodus. According to the story, in remembrance of the fact that God passed over the homes of the Israelites that were appropriately blood-stained, God then decides to claim the firstborn of every Israelite woman, sheep, and cow as God's own. But, Moses proclaims that there is an out for the human babies. They may be redeemed through the offering of a ritually pure firstborn of another species.

I never have understood why God is so often portrayed as being in need of some sort of ultimate sacrifice in order to be appeased. I wonder if it might be an attempt at explaining what must surely have been a fairly high infant mortality rate. Whatever the case, the sacrifice is required, and the means to avoid it are described plainly.

It just goes to show that even a warrior God, as God is often portrayed in the Hebrew scriptures, is still a God of compassion and grace. God goes out of the way to make sure that even God's own decrees are not always followed if to do so might cause undue harm or death to an innocent.

Testing: 1 ... 2 ... 3 ...

"Do not put the Lord your God to the test ..." (Deuteronomy 6:16)

I very greatly dislike taking tests. No matter the subject about which I am being tested or the form of the test, I don't like being tested. Put one of those things in front of me and my brain locks up so tightly that Houdini couldn't escape it. No matter that I probably know more than the test might ask of me, I go into mental meltdown. I thought about becoming a real estate broker one time. I took an 80-classroom hour class to prepare and received a grade of "A". But, to get the license, I had to pass a 100-question test. I tried three times, and failed three times.

Of course, there are other kinds of tests which take very different forms. Right now I'm nearing the end of the first year of a test that will last, I'm guessing, for quite a few more years. I am the father of a teenager. The language she now speaks on most days is not English, it's Estrogen. Can you explain to me how telling her she looks nice in the morning turns into an examination of 1) the quality of my eyesight, 2) my knowledge of proper parenting since no parent would ever persecute their child by telling the child he or she looks nice when it is so obvious that this is not the case or, 3) my understanding of cosmetic application since I would not think she looks nice if I knew how her make-up was supposed to look. Like I said before, I don't like being tested.

I don't like being tested, but the author of Deuteronomy gives the impression that God simply won't put up with it. And yet, people test God constantly. Who among us has not caught ourselves saying, "I'll tell you what, God; You do this for me, and I'll do that for you." Even as we say it, we know that we have no intention of keeping our part of the bargain. It's just a test to see if God can get enough of the matching and true/false questions right to pass. I really don't think it's a good idea to give God a test. In fact, I think God is probably partial to essays in which God focuses on the folly of being tested..

"I'll take 'Unwise Choices' for $500, Alex."

Let the Good Times Roll!

Hezekiah ... prayed for them, saying, "The good Lord pardon all who set their hearts to seek God, the Lord the God of their ancestors, even though not in accordance with the sanctuary's rules of cleanness ..." The people ate the food of the festival for seven days ... Then the whole assembly agreed to keep the festival for another seven days. (II Chronicles 30:18, 22-23)

I loved church camp when I was a young lad. Mostly, I liked the experiences because they marked the first times when I was allowed to be anywhere that my parents weren't. Also, there were lots of girls there who didn't know me and hadn't already figured out what a nerd I was. Hope sprang eternal! On the other hand, the leadership of those camp events was skilled at bringing youngsters from diverse backgrounds and locations together as a community in a really short period of time. Thus, I was never appreciative of the arrival of Saturday morning which meant I would be returning to the watchful eye of my parents and to all those girls who already knew me. Bummer! Why couldn't we just stay for two weeks instead of only one?

There were apparently quite a few people who weren't particularly interested in what Hezekiah was doing to bring the nation back into a good relationship with God. On the other hand, there were many who were *very* interested. They couldn't wait to get to Jerusalem and let the Passover party begin! Some of them were so anxious to get the ball rolling that they walked right to the table and dished themselves up some boiled lamb with mint jelly without first washing their hands 37 times, or whatever it was they were supposed to do in order to be "sanctified." Now as you can imagine, the keepers of the law, were simply aghast at this breech of ceremonial etiquette.

Hezekiah pondered the situation for a bit and decided that, in the grand scheme of things, having people anxious to resume their relationship with God took precedent over how many times they washed their hands before they ate. So, most likely in a public forum of some sort, Hezekiah prayed a prayer, honestly seeking God's good will, but also as a means of placating all who heard it. The prayer apparently had the intended effect. After everybody had been partying for a week, somebody said, "I don't want to go home yet." Somebody else said, "Me, neither." The next thing you know, everybody decides that if one week of Passover partying is good, two surely has to be even better. Thus, they stayed.

I sometimes think of this story on Sunday morning when folks start stealing furtive glances at their watches if the preacher (that would be me) starts getting long-winded, i.e., talking for more than fifteen minutes. I think it would be fun some Sunday at the end of the proceedings, for someone to stand up and say, "Wow, this was so cool. Let's stay and do it some more!" I don't see it happening any time soon, but it *would* be fun.

Let's Get Even

"Repay (the wicked) according to their work, and according to the evil of their deeds; repay them according to the work of their hands; render them their due reward." (Psalm 28:4)

I let Virgil Turner use my ball glove in third grade during recess. When the bell rang, he dropped it on the playground and ran. I had to go get it, was late to class, and got in trouble. I went home that night, and delivered my plea for vengeance to Mother. I wanted her to go right to that school the next day, box Virgil Turner's ears, and tell that teacher exactly how things work in the world. Instead, she said, "Maybe you need to think first before you let people borrow your ball glove."

That wasn't the right response at all! I wanted vengeance; I wanted retaliation; I wanted there to be consequences. Instead, I heard about the importance of making wise choices.

In the verse I quoted above, we have a part of a prayer hymn written by none other than David himself. It's a cheerful little ditty to sing on the Sabbath, don't you think? I might re-write it something like this:

"To those who are mean to me, give them their due;
They have been evil to me and to You.
As they have given, may now they receive;
To their own devices, O Lord, please now leave."

I suppose there may be some way to understand the thinking here. David was a warrior king. His fame began on a battle field, and he had spent a lot of time there in the intervening years. Not only that, due to some of his personal choices, he had made enemies among his own people along with all of his battle foes. To understand then, that he might feel a bit put upon, and that he might feel that a little revenge is in order, does not take an incredibly great stretch of the imagination.

Why is it, though, that people seem to assume that their enemies are God's enemies, too? That's a leap of logic I just can't make. Have they forgotten that all of creation is God's handiwork? The thing is, as much as it might disappoint many people, God is a God of love, not vengeance. It is an affront to God to expect that He/She should take our side every time we make somebody mad.

Trusting in the Power of Green Stamps

"Into Your hand I commit my spirit; you have redeemed me, O Lord ..."
(Psalm 31:5)

When I was young, every Friday when Mother went to the grocery store, she'd come home with sacks full of groceries (often including a bag full of these nasty-tasting yellow candy peanuts!), and a fist full of yellow stamps. In some parts of the grocery-buying world, the stamps were green; they served the same purpose regardless of color. There were these books that one could also get into which the stamps were to be licked and glued. Ultimately these books of stamps could be "redeemed" for various and sundry types of merchandise. For three books of stamps, one could get some plastic leftover containers. For 25,643 books of stamps one could get a new Ford. It all depended on what you had to redeem. Every time I read in the book about somebody being redeemed by God, this image blazes across the landscape of my mind of God sauntering up with 500 or 600 books of stamps and saying, "I'd like to redeem a 95-year-old man in South Dakota, please."

Then there's the first phrase in verse 5: "Into Your hands I commit my spirit." David must have read somewhere that Jesus said that when he was dying, and so thought he would put it in one of his songs. No wait; Jesus didn't die until later, did he? Anyway, this little seven-word statement indicates something very scary. How willing are you to totally entrust your very life to someone else? Even more so, can you entrust your spirit to someone else? I don't know if I can. People continually betray my trust. I've been lied to, lied about, slandered, discriminated against, and ignored; and that's just by the people I thought liked me and were worthy of my trust. That being the case, it seems to me that what David says here, and what Jesus repeated a few hundred years later, must be one of the greatest statements of faith ever made. If it is difficult to trust those we can see; how is it possible to trust Someone we can't see?

146

The only answer I have for that question is that, so far as I know, God has never betrayed my trust. I'm getting to the point where I'm starting to think God just might succeed in never betraying my trust. That being the case, if I have to commit my spirit into anyone's hands, it might as well be God.

Taking Refuge in the Spare Bedroom

"... happy are those who take refuge in (the Lord)." (Psalm 34:8)

I live an interesting life. I spend my weekdays at a high school where I take part in the education of young people who live with various kinds of developmental and behavioral exceptionalities. I love everything about this process; and by the end of the day I am exhausted. I then come home and assume the mantel of college instructor as I teach courses in world religion and cultural diversity for an online, virtual university. I love everything about this process and by the time I turn the computer off at 8:00 p.m., I'm exhausted. I am in the eleventh year of being the part-time pastor of a little community of folks 80 miles from where I live. I get up at 5:00 a.m. on Sunday morning, drive for an hour and a half, share worship with them, visit in their homes, and return home in the late afternoon. I love everything about this process, and when I get home on Sunday afternoon, I'm exhausted. I have lived for 25 years with the most wonderful woman in the world. I don't think it would be possible for two people to have such completely opposite personalities. I love everything about the process of being married to her, and there are days when working at our marriage leaves us both exhausted. I have two fantastic daughters. One is 23 years old and lives with several developmental and emotional exceptionalities. I love everything about the process of being her father, and that process often leaves me exhausted. My other daughter is 14 years old. I love everything about the process of being her father, and that process often leaves me exhausted. After all, as I mentioned, she is 14 years old.

My computer is located in the spare bedroom of our house. Most often when I am working the door stands open so that wife, daughters, dog and cat know they are welcome to join me. However, there are days when circumstances lead me to close the door. When I do wife, daughters and dog will hopefully understand that the room has become my place of refuge. The cat doesn't care; if he wants in he'll rub his clawless paws on the door incessantly.

Every human being needs a refuge. It is an essential ingredient for good mental, emotional, and spiritual health. In the psalm, David assures us that even when we can't close the door to the spare bedroom, still we can find refuge in knowing that God watches over us.

"… happy are those who take refuge in (the Lord)."

Do Dogs Have a Purpose?

"… You save humans and animals alike, O Lord." (Psalm 36:6)

After about a day and a half of my unplanned early retirement, my house got too quiet once my wife and oldest daughter left for work and the young one went to school. The cat was around, but he wasn't having much to do with me at the time. I decided that what I needed was a dog. Not just any dog; a Pomeranian like my Grandma Thomas had when I was a wee lad. So I got on the internet and found a Pomeranian in a shelter. I was going to name him Old Bob, and he would ride in the van with me when I went places and he would be my best friend. Well, I went to pick up the dog and as soon as I got to the shelter, the caretaker said, "His name is Stewart, and he will not answer to anything else." Stewart? Stewart? Who in the world would name a dog Stewart? I got him in the van and we started home. I said to him, "Stewart is no name for a manly dog like you." To which he responded with that irritating Pomeranian yip that the years had erased from my memory. For a week, I called him Old Bob. For that same week, he ignored me. However, the three women with whom I live all thought that Stewart was the perfect name for such a precious little bundle of canine cuteness. So, when they weren't listening, I asked him, "Do you really like being called 'Stewart'?" To which he yipped at a decibel level rivaled only by the noise at a Grateful Dead concert I went to one time. Then he jumped into my lap and started licking my face.

Well, times have changed. My physical opportunities now have a name; the doctors have come up with some strategies that make the situation tolerable, and I went and found a part time job at the high school. When that happened I figured it was time to find the dog a better place to live since I wouldn't be around as much as I had intended when I first brought him home. You would have thought that I announced to my wife and daughters that we would be subsisting on a diet of spinach for a month the way they howled and moaned when I said the dog had to go. So, three years later Stewart is still here, he still yips that irritating yip, and I'm the one who takes him out in the middle of the night.

What does this have to do with the statement David makes about God saving humans and animals? Probably nothing except that in the case of this tiny ball of aggravation at our house, my wife and daughters have apparently become God's incarnation. Every time I mention the quite practical reality that he needs to live somewhere else, they step right up and save his sorry hide one more time.

I wonder what God was thinking by allowing people to come up with such an irritatingly obnoxious version of the dog. God must have been off exploding a super nova in a galaxy far, far away the day that happened.

What Happens When Our Foot Slips?

"I pray, 'Only do not let them rejoice over me, those who boast against me when my foot slips." (Psalm 38:16)

You may recall a few years ago when the President of the United States underwent some pretty intense scrutiny when it was revealed that he had redefined the job description for one of his summer interns. Everybody from the local grocery store clerk to heads of state in other countries had a field day boasting against him when his foot slipped. Now, I'm not defending the man or his actions for a minute. I'll not be his judge, either. It just goes to show that people always take perverse pleasure in seeing the humanity of those in positions of leadership laid bare. That, I think, is unfair.

It was happening to David, as well. He was a pretty good king, as kings go; he was also all too human. Further, he didn't do much to hide his personal life from his adoring public. So, people were taking potshots at him all the time. It seems that he had resigned himself to this so he figured that at least God might give him a break. They might be snickering behind his back, but David figures that the least God can do is make sure they don't enjoy the snickering they're doing.

That's the way it goes, isn't it? We mess up, people make fun of us, and we get mad. If we're little children, we most likely run home to mommy. "Mommy, I fell down and got my new dress dirty and Jessie laughed at me. Will you call her mom?" A little later, it's "Dad, I know I promised I'd be careful with the combine, but I accidentally backed over the lawn tractor with it, and Brad said I'll never be a farmer. Is it OK if I knock his lights out?"

Hopefully not many of us will find ourselves in the position that our former President did; nonetheless, throughout life the circumstances change but the scenario doesn't. It seems to me that the process might go a little smoother if we could learn to admit when we err, face whatever consequences are to be faced, and then laugh with everyone else.

Special Delivery

"I have told the glad news of deliverance ... I have spoken of (God's) salvation." (Psalm 40:9-10)

After Dad and several relatives remodeled our house back in the late 1950s, it became a bi-level dwelling; actually I think the term was split-level. A hole was dug and a garage constructed on the east end of the house with two bedrooms built on top of it. Both the basement and the bedrooms were offset from the original structure. Anyway, when all was said and done, there was a new incline in our back yard down to the garage door.

Not long after the completion of this architectural masterpiece, Dad also made the momentous decision that he needed some help keeping the yard mowed and that I was just the man to provide that assistance. We had a little 24 inch riding lawnmower that Dad taught me to use. I want to tell you, I thought I was destined to become a legend at Talladega, so confident did I become in my operation of that awesome piece of machinery.

One day, while performing my landscaping wizardry in the back yard, I noticed a small patch of as yet unmowed grass. Not to worry, I threw that mower into reverse so as to better align me and my machine with the aforementioned patch. I paid no attention to the fact that I was less than a foot from the incline leading down to the garage door. I released the clutch and promptly started over the incline backwards. In the next split second, the front wheels came off the ground. In the split second after that, one incredibly strong hand attached to an even stronger arm attached itself to the steering handle and forced the front of the mower back to the ground. At the bottom of the incline, I received an impromptu, yet forceful, lesson regarding the importance of always being aware of my surroundings when operating any type of motorized conveyance. That I did not receive the right hand of fellowship on my behind came as a major shock to me. However, what I knew was that I had been delivered by the closest thing to God with which I was acquainted at the time. I was frightened and embarrassed. Nonetheless, I said "thank you" in as many different ways as I could think of. Believe me when I say that I spoke of the salvation I had received.

Over the years since that fateful day, I have been delivered from my own fool-ishness more times than I can even remember. Once or twice, I have wondered why God continues to bother. The thing is that's really none of my business. So, the best I can do is to keep right on speaking of God's salvation.

What is Trust?

"Even my bosom friend in whom I trusted, who ate of my bread, has lifted the heel against me." (Psalm 41:9, 12)

Several years ago, Roxanne and I developed a really nice friendship with the organist at the church where I was working at the time. He was not a church member, nor did he live in the community. He was a "hired gun" who came in on Sunday morning, did his musical thing, collected his paycheck, and left. Anyway, we seemed to have quite a bit in common and so, as I said, a nice friendship developed. We did many things together socially, and it was fun spending time with him.

It was during this time that my Grandpa Sinclair died (he was the first of my grandparents to do so). The organist was right there beside me through that experience; even traveling to Indiana with Roxanne and me for the memorial. I was quite thankful for his compassion and availability.

About a year and a half later, for reasons that I do not understand to this day, this man betrayed my confidence more totally and completely than I could have imagined possible. When confronted with his betrayal, he readily admitted what he had done but acted as though it was the most natural thing in the world and indicated that he couldn't understand why I should be bothered. I spent many sleepless nights trying to understand what had motivated his actions, but understanding did not come. Roxanne and I mulled it over and over and over and wound up frustrated. As a consequence, my trust in human beings was reduced to a state of near imperceptibility. Fifteen years later, any new person I meet has to assume that I don't trust them until they have earned my trust.

I really don't like feeling that way; but there it is. It is just plain hard to open yourself up to someone when that little voice in the back of your head keeps saying, "Don't trust; don't trust; don't trust."

When it comes right down to it, I have to believe as David did; listen to the 12th verse of this Psalm: "… But God has upheld me because of my integrity, and set me in (God's) presence forever." Sometimes, we just have to try and remember that God *will* uphold us when no one else will.

155

Where Does God Use Me?

"These things I remember as I pour out my soul; how I went with the throng and led them in procession to the house of God, with glad songs of thanksgiving, a multitude keeping festival. Why are you cast down, O my soul, and why are you disquieted within me?" (Psalm 42:4-5)

In the summer of 1974, I was asked to sing with a group of college guys who called themselves The New World Committee. I was still in the Air Force, and hadn't even started college yet. But, the bass guitar player and I had been at a conference at the same time and he had heard me pick and sing. Based on his recommendation, I was invited to join. The very first engagement at which the group was to perform after I joined was the Southern Illinois Conference of the United Methodist Church's annual youth event. Up until this time, I had sung for maybe 50 people on one or two occasions. As I walked into the auditorium of the high school in Mt. Vernon, Illinois on that Sunday afternoon in November, I looked out and saw about 600 faces staring back at me! Talk about nervous?! Well, we launched into the first tune which was a hand-clapping, knee-slapping little ditty. In no time, the young people were on their feet, swinging and swaying. They gave us a standing ovation after every song we sang. What a party! What a rush! What an emotional high I was on! The best part was that everyone was there because God meant something to them.

On Monday I put the uniform back on and went back to work as Sgt. Sinclair. My soul was cast down; it was disquieted within me. After having led the people in "glad shouts and songs of thanksgiving," there I was back doing the same old same old.

There are times in our lives when it seems like God gives us opportunities to do God's work in venues which will produce that emotional and spiritual high I felt in that auditorium. I think we need to be thankful for those times when they happen. We also need to realize that on Monday we'll most likely be back doing what we were doing before. We need to guard against those feelings that the psalmist and I felt. We need to realize that God uses us more often in the same old same old than anywhere else. Besides, there is no end to opportunities to praise God, if we will just be open to all of them.

God Needs a Day Off

"I say to God, my rock, 'Why have You forgotten me, why must I walk around mournfully ...? 'My adversaries taunt me, while they say to me continually, 'Where is your God?'" (Psalm 42:9-10)

Do you suppose God ever takes a day off? Really, now think about it. Doing all that God stuff day in and day out, week after week, month after month, year after year, decade after decade, century after century, eon after eon must make God at least a little tired. I would think that every three or four million years, God might just like to grab the tackle box and the fishing pull and head off to the lake for five or six nanoseconds. The only thing about that thought that bothers me is the fear of thinking God might go fishing without me.

Whether God takes a day off or not, most folks experience times when it certainly seems as though God has stepped out of the office for a moment or three. They think they've earned the right to expect God to come bounding up like an excited puppy whenever they whistle. When that doesn't happen, then they think that God has abandoned them. They're like a child in the woods who wanders off from Mom or Dad and the sun starts to set. They look around, can't figure out where they are, and think Mom or Dad abandoned *them*! They think it was Mom or Dad who wandered off.

God doesn't go wandering; God is pretty steadfast and constant. So then, what are people to conclude when, like the psalmist, God doesn't seem to be in the vicinity? It seems to me they might conclude that, since God hasn't gone anywhere, then maybe they have. It could be that they've wandered off in the woods at sunset. When that happens, God being God and all, the fishing trip is stopped short and God goes looking just like any good parent would do.

I've decided; God does need a day off. So, the second Tuesday of week after next, God and I are going fishing. You all might want to plan accordingly.

It's Not God's Fault

"Because of You, we are being killed all day long … Rouse Yourself; why do You sleep, O Lord?" (Psalm 44:22-23)

Back in the 1960s, comedian Flip Wilson had an alter-ego named Geraldine. Geraldine could get herself into more mischief than should be possible for one human being. When asked to provide rationale for her behavior, the response was always the same—"The devil made me do it!" She never did take responsibility for her actions. It was far easier to pin the blame on some contrived cosmic consciousness which, of course, could not provide any defense.

As if you couldn't tell, the same person is still whining to God here in Psalm 44 as was in Psalm 42. Things are really not going at all like the psalmist wants and so he does what any good human being in a bit of trouble would do—he or she blames the devil. No, wait; that's not right; she or he blames God. Now there's something else I just don't get. Why is it that, whenever things start to get really smelly, we almost always blame God? We get ourselves into all kinds of mischief and then when we need an explanation the response is: "It's God's fault." What a bunch of nonsense.

The psalmist is actually pretty brave, or pretty stupid. Can you imagine having the sheer audacity to tell God that it's God's fault people are dying. And then to follow that up by saying, "Hey, You! Wake up! What gives here? You're supposed to be taking care of business but it looks to me like You're taking a nap instead." That is sort of like walking up to the boss and saying, "Look, the workers on the line have been goofing off, production is down, and the corporation is talking about layoffs. It's all your fault." If you were God, wouldn't you be tempted just a little bit to chuck a lightening bolt or two?

When people get themselves into uncomfortable situations, when nations get themselves into wars, it's not God's fault. Just leave God out of it, place the blame where it belongs, and take care of it.

Oops!

"Have mercy on me, O God, according to Your steadfast love; according to Your abundant mercy blot out my transgressions." (Psalm 51:1)

Fast forward about 3000 years and this song which we read as Psalm 51 would probably been a million seller by some teeny bopper. Wait a minute! That actually happened! Some teeny bopper did it a few years ago. I don't remember the exact words, but the title was something like, "Oops, I Did It Again." I suppose by now you're thinking, "What in the world is he talking about this time?"

You may remember from your adult Sunday school class about some of King David's escapades. Some of them were rated R for nudity, sex, and gratuitous violence and so no one under the age of 17 was aloud to study them. It seems that one day, David was standing out on the balcony drinking his second cup of morning coffee when over in the next block he happened to see a really beautiful woman doing some sunbathing—without any clothes on! Being the good king that he was, David thought to himself, "I think I would like for her to meet me for lunch." So, he sent for his bowl, he sent for his pipe, he sent for his lyre-players three. He pointed out the lovely sunbather to them, and one of the musicians said, "Begging the King's pardon, but her name is Bathsheba, and she's already married. To which David replied, "What is that to me? I'm the king!" To which another lyre-player responded, "Well, it's not quite that simple. She's married to Uriah." Uriah the Hittite was the only five-star general in David's army at the time. Being ever resourceful, David sent out an executive order to Uriah telling him to report immediately to the front lines. Being a career soldier, Uriah did what he was told and was promptly killed as reward. Then David sent a driver over to pick up Bathsheba. The king and the grieving widow then spent the afternoon in connubial bliss.

The community prophet at the time was a guy named Nathan. When he saw Bathsheba leaving the palace the next morning and looking quite disheveled, he marched himself right up to the king's private quarters, barged in without knocking, and told David exactly what he thought of his most recent round of decision-making.

I share all of that with you to explain this Psalm. After Nathan got through with the king, David started to think, "Surely God's not mad at me just because I arranged a man's death and spent the afternoon with his widow!" But then he thought, "Just to be on the safe side, I'd better write a new song." So he took out quill and parchment, and composed Psalm 51. "Have mercy on me, O God; … blot out my transgressions." See what I meant when I said the psalm could have been titled, "Oops!"

Folks still do things the way David did. They have their party, and give no consideration to the consequences until the next morning. Once the searing reality sinks in, then they're on their knees saying, "Oops, sorry about that, God!" As if saying "Oops" will make it all better. The really disturbing thing is that God appears to be someone for whom "Oops" just might make it all better. That's what forgiveness is all about. Now, that's not to say that people we offend will forget or that we will forget those who offend us. But, true forgiveness transcends all human emotion. True forgiveness is the only thing I know of that makes emotional healing possible.

Bird Sanctuary

"He will cover you with his pinions; and under his wings you will find refuge." (Psalm 91:4)

The other night, some friends came over to our house with a movie they wanted to watch with us. I'll bet that many of you have seen it. The movie is basically a documentary about the lives of Emperor Penguins who live in Antarctica. The penguins live an interesting life. They spend several months in the ocean waters eating and eating and eating. Then as winter approaches they go ashore and walk seventy miles to the place where they meet and mate. If the process is successful and an egg is produced by a "meet and mate" couple, something very interesting happens. The momma and daddy will perform an elaborate ritual in which the egg is transferred from the momma to the daddy. Once this is successfully accomplished, the momma walks the seventy miles back to the ocean, eats her fill, and walks the seventy miles back so she can feed her baby. Meanwhile, for the several weeks that process takes, dad is back home covering the egg with his pinions. Actually, dad has a specially designed roll of skin with which he covers the egg to keep it warm during the Antarctic winter.

What fascinated me about the whole thing is that in the case of many if not most members of the animal kingdom, it is the mother who is responsible for nurturing the young. In the case of these incredible birds, that role falls to the father. Thus I was really intrigued to find these words in Psalm 91 where the psalmist likens God to a father bird. "He will cover you with his pinions, and under his wings you will find refuge." I don't know what other species of bird features the father as nurturer, but there must be some because the image impressed the writer of this psalm so much that he would use it to describe God.

Of course, at another place in the Hebrew Scriptures, God is likened to a mother eagle guarding her young. Put those two images together and you have a God I can feel pretty safe with. Being guarded and kept safe under the wings. That's right cozy, don't you think?

Count Your Calamities; Name
Them One By One

*"Give thanks to the Lord, for He is good: … His steadfast love endures for-
ever. Let the redeemed of the Lord say so." (Psalm 107:1-2)*

Every once in a while, if I'm not paying close enough attention, I find myself
being distracted by what I perceive to be my great litany of problematic situations. I mean, just listen to this. I have a mortgage I have to pay every month. In
the last four years, my body has fallen apart; my neck is held together with tita-
nium plates and screws, I have developed a neuromuscular disease that makes me
hurt somewhere every minute of every hour of every day of every week of every
year. I have double vision. The dependability of my left leg is questionable at
best. As I write this, I have one daughter who is in love for the first time in her
life. I have another daughter who has just begun her teen years and is under the
total and absolute sway of hormones. I am married to a woman who is as theologically and ideologically different from me as it is conceivably possible to be.
Finally, I live hundreds of miles from my parents and my siblings. How much
worse can one life get?

The thing of it is, every one of these personal calamities which I have just
shared with you is, to a far greater extent, proof of just how good God is to me.
My mortgage means that I have a house to live in. That's pretty nice once cold
weather sets in. My poor, pathetic excuse for a body is evidence that I am still
waking up alive each morning, having been given that gift by God one more
time. The fact that I have daughters who challenge me on a continual basis is evidence that I have been given another of the greatest gifts any man can receive: I
get to be a father. The mystery that is the woman to whom I have been married
for twenty-five years is yet another of God's great gifts. She constantly challenges
me to be the best I can be. She cares for me when I'm sick; she holds me when
I'm sad; she kicks my butt when I'm obnoxious. She is my life's companion. The
fact that I live hundreds of miles from my parents and siblings is evidence that I

have parents and siblings. My wife is an only child whose father and mother have both died in the recent past.

"Give thanks to the Lord, for He is good: ... His steadfast love endures forever. Let the redeemed of the Lord say so."

That's the Thanks You Get

"I give You thanks, O Lord, with my whole heart … for Your steadfast love and faithfulness." (Psalm 138:1-2)

A few years ago, I wrote my own version of this psalm. The chorus goes like this:

"Thank You for being there when I grow tired;
When I'm weary, and want to cave in.
You give me the power to go on one more hour,
And get ready to serve you again."

"Thank you." Now here are two little words when put together are worth more than all the gold in all the vaults in all the countries of the world. These are also two little words that aren't put together nearly often enough, to my way of thinking.

If our mommas and daddies raised us right, they taught us to say "please" when requesting something and "thank you" when receiving something. To do so is considered a sign of good manners in most polite societies. It appears that some of us learn our manners, or at least learn to express them, better than others.

However, learning to say "thank you" on the obvious occasions is not that difficult a skill to master in the grand scheme of things. On the other hand, how many of us remember to say "thank you" when our life is in the toilet and circumstances are getting ready to flip the flush handle? For that matter, why would anybody be so dumb as to assert that there is anything to say "thank you" for when we are swimming in the great commode of life? Why, indeed.

I'll tell you why. Actually, I'll let the author of Psalm 138 tell you: "Though I walk in the midst of trouble, You stretch out Your hand and Your right hand delivers me." That's why.

I don't know about you, but it is in those yucky times that God steps up and reminds me that I'm not facing anything alone. I'm a pretty ungrateful old sap if I can't say thank you for that!

The God of the Obstinate

"… I know that you are obstinate, and your neck is an iron sinew, and your forehead brass." (Isaiah 48:4)

Every once in a while, on one of those rare occasions when I am absolutely, positively certain that I am right about something and I deflect all attempts to persuade me otherwise, my spouse has a tendency to look my way and exclaim, "Ed, you old bullhead!" (This is *not* the same thing as a knot-head.) I had to live with her for fifteen or twenty years before I figured out that she wasn't paying me a compliment. You see, in so addressing me, Roxanne is speaking in her native Iowegian tongue and is using phraseology with which I had been heretofore unfamiliar. It turns out that she is saying, "Ed, you are obstinate, your neck is an iron sinew, and your forehead brass." Now, why didn't she just say that in the first place?

By the time of the Babylonian Captivity, as this period in Israel's history is named by some historians, God has been putting up with more grief and aggravation from "the Chosen" than any parent should have to endure. If, as the stories would have us believe, these people truly were somehow chosen by God, they've not done much to show their gratitude. They are ornery, they are contrary, and they make idols out of gold or an old tree stump whenever they think God is not looking. Still God keeps bailing their behinds out of scrape after scrape. It seems as though they just never quite seem to get it right.

All I can say is, thank God for the people of Israel and for the stories we have of God's relationship with them. No matter what kind of messes they get themselves into, God is steadfast. God hangs in there when God's patience must be worn completely out.

It is reassuring to know that, when Roxanne thinks I'm an "old bullhead," God still loves me.

Did God Forget Something?

Zion said, "The Lord has forsaken me; my Lord has forgotten me." "Can a woman forget her nursing child, or show no compassion for the child of her womb? Even these may forget, yet I will not forget you ..." (Isaiah 49:14-15)

This is an interesting analogy. God is likened to a nursing mother and a pregnant woman. You don't see *that* every day.

After Cristina was born and we were finally able to bring her home (she was three months premature and stayed in the hospital for six weeks) natural feeding was not successful. Thus, Roxanne and I took turns feeding her specially prepared formula. Every three hours around the clock we took turns feeding her. I remember being really tired most of the time. I don't remember minding at all. Further, I don't remember ever forgetting to feed her. That's just something a parent doesn't seem to forget.

For many reasons, Roxanne's pregnancy was a touch and go proposition from start to finish. Every night before we went to sleep, we each placed a hand on her tummy and said a prayer for the new life trying hard to grow in there. That she had conceived and was carrying a child was a miracle for many reasons. We both felt unending compassion for that tiny little person who was yet to be born.

The Jews in Babylon felt, perhaps with some justification, that God had forgotten them. After all the covenants God had made with their ancestors; with Noah, and Abraham, and Isaac, and Moses, God had forgotten them, or so they thought. "We wouldn't be in this predicament if God remembered us," was their line of reasoning. So, Second Isaiah, once again speaking for God, assures them that God does not forget. God operates according to some sort of eternal timetable unknown to humankind, but God does not forget.

There were a few times when Roxanne and I were on the verge of thinking maybe we had slipped God's mind. When that little two pound bundle of energy started breathing on her own within an hour after she was born, we were reassured.

People might forget God; in fact, people *do* forget God. No matter; God does not forget us. Ever.

Home is Where the Hat Is

"Shake yourself from the dust, rise up, … loose the bonds from your neck, O captive daughter Zion … Depart, depart, go out from there! Touch no unclean thing; go out from the midst of it, purify yourselves, you who carry the vessels of the Lord…. For the Lord will go before you, and the God of Israel will be your rear guard." (Isaiah 52:2, 11-12)

Home; what a powerful little four-letter word. It describes something everyone longs for. Some always have it and never leave it. Some have it, leave it, and go back to it. Some leave it, and never go back. Some have never had it. I happen to be one who left it, and never went back. That wasn't the plan; not at all. On August 31, 1971, I got on a Greyhound bus that I thought was headed for Indianapolis. The truth is; I'm not sure where that bus ride is taking me because it has never ended. When I left Mother and Dad at the bus station that evening, I had every intention of going back home as soon as possible. I was on my way to Air Force basic training in San Antonio, Texas. My plan was then to try to get stationed at Grissom Air Force Base which was about 40 miles from the house I grew up in. During the third week of basic training, I had the opportunity fill out a "dream sheet" on which I listed the three state-side bases where I would most like to be, and one overseas base of my choosing. I had heard through the grapevine that I should no way put my first choice at the top of my list because I would not get my first choice under any circumstances. So, I put a place I'd never heard of called Scott Air Force Base, which is in southern Illinois at the top of the list. After completing technical school in Mississippi, I was stationed at a place I'd never heard of called Scott Air Force Base in southern Illinois. I never went back to Indiana to live.

In 1986, Mother and Dad sold the place in which they had raised me, the place where I had spent most of my first 19 years, and moved to their retreat in the southern Indiana hills. At that point, I realized that I couldn't go home if I wanted to because home belonged to someone else.

I also began to realize that home is what and where I choose it to be. That being the case, that Greyhound bus has made stops in Illinois, Ohio, Kansas, Missouri, Iowa, and now Illinois again. Somehow or another, I've been able to find some sense of home at each of those stops on the trip. I think I've figured out why that is. The Lord has gone before me, and God has been my rear guard. That's way more reassuring than any of those feeble human-made attempts at security.

Shake It Up, Israelites; Sing and Shout!

"Sing, O barren one who did not bear; burst into song and shout, you who have not been in labor! For the children of the desolate woman will be more that the children of her that is married," says the Lord. (Isaiah 54:1)

Roxanne and I were married when we were both 29 years old. She was about to begin her seminary indoctrination, so our first priority was to get her through that ordeal and still be married at the end of it all. With that goal accomplished, we turned our attention to the propagation of the species. However, our efforts proved futile for quite a while. We had just about given up on the whole notion when, at the age of 38, Roxanne became pregnant. Our joy knew no bounds! Twelve weeks later, she experienced a miscarriage. It was then that the doctor told us not to try that again because of some irregularities in Roxanne's reproductive system. We felt like the barren ones to whom Pseudo-Isaiah addresses his words. In fact, we felt pretty sorry for ourselves.

Nonetheless, life went on and, after talking about it and praying about it, we decided to adopt a child. As a result of a long and complicated series of events, we learned about the little one named Maria who lived in an orphanage in Ecuador and who was to become our daughter. In December 1991 we received the paperwork informing us that we had been approved to become Maria's parents. We began to cautiously sing and shout at this good news, even though we had not been in labor. The day after we received that paperwork in the mail, I got home from a meeting to see the light on the answering machine blinking. Roxanne had left a message indicating that she had interesting news. When she returned home, she revealed that she was once again pregnant. Our joy became mixed with fear.

In the meantime, we continued with our preparations to make Maria a member of our family. This included making a two-week trip to Ecuador and preparing our home for a young child. Maria finally came to our home on March 20, 1992. On June 13, when Roxanne was barely six months into her pregnancy, she went into labor. Three days later, Cristina was born, weighing in at 2 pounds 9 ounces. In less than three months, we had gone from being childless to having two daughters.

As the Israelites still held captive in Babylon were about to discover, the exile was almost over. They were going home and would become prodigious in their creation of offspring. Roxanne and I were certainly not prodigious, but we were privileged to have the opportunity to sing and shout because of God's goodness to us.

The Banes of Bocock Road

"Let the wicked forsake their way and the unrighteous their thoughts; let them return to the Lord who will have mercy on them, and to our God who will abundantly pardon." (Isaiah 55:7)

The Stevens brothers, Danny, David, and Carey, were the Banes of Bocock Road. If the tracks would have crossed that road, the Stevens brothers would have been from the other side of them. They were rough, they were tough, they were mean and most of the rest of us trembled at the sight of any one of them.

The creek ran through the middle of the home place, turned north and formed the east boundary of the property. At the northeast edge of the woods, the creek ran under the Bocock Road bridge. Danny and David, the two older of the Stevens brothers, had a group of compatriots with whom they started gathering under the bridge to have a smoke and tell stories. Dad got wind of the fact that they were there about the third time they congregated. He was concerned because technically they had to walk across the edge of our place to get under the bridge. Dad had this thing about trespassers, you see. So, after supper that third evening he took a walk down to the bridge. He was gone a long time! Finally we heard not just Dad's voice approaching the house, but several voices. What should our apprehensive eyes behold but Dad, Danny, David, and a couple of their buddies headed for the back door! Once inside, Dad got out his prized 1956 Gibson ES-225 (that's a guitar, folks) and handed it to Danny Stevens! Then he suggested that I get my 1961 Gibson Les Paul Junior (that's another guitar). Danny looked at me and said, "Do you know how to play?" "A little bit," escaped from my trembling lips. We then proceeded to play every song we knew for about the next hour. After that day, the Stevens brothers acted as my "slack;" my "back up." I played guitar; I was cool.

Those boys were the most wicked of the wicked as far as most folks were concerned. Dad went to confront them that day because of their reputation. What happened instead was that they received mercy and, I dare say, even pardon. Dad discovered a common ground and used it to make the Stevens brothers feel like human beings instead of outcasts. There were a lot of folks who didn't trust the bond that developed at all. It didn't matter; what mattered was how those brothers responded to being treated decently.

Imagine then, if you will, how the upright Israelites must have felt upon hearing Second Isaiah pronounce that God's goodness would be extending not only to them, but to the wicked as well. I'll bet a few of them said, "Who does God think He is; God?" That was most likely *exactly* who God thought God was.

But Who Will Forgive Me?

"O Lord, hear; O Lord, forgive; O Lord, listen and act and do not delay!
For Your own sake, O my God." (Daniel 9:19)

I knew a Presbyterian pastor whose spouse committed suicide. At a conference not long thereafter, he and I and several other folks were sitting in a hotel room telling stories. At about 2:00 in the morning, my Presbyterian colleague started to weep and then his grief came rushing out in a torrent of torment. He talked for a very long time about his life with his spouse; how, like every marriage, theirs had its ups and downs. He shared about how she had battled clinical depression for many years. He even talked about the horror of returning home to find her lying in their bed with several empty medication bottles nearby. He then told us that he should have read the signs better. He was certain that he could have brought about a different outcome if he had been more diligent. But ... now she was gone, he was alone, and he still had difficulty facing his congregation because he knew that they knew. Finally, he admitted how angry he was at her for abandoning him.

After he had talked himself out, the room was quiet for several minutes. Finally, one of our other friends walked over to the pastor, put his hand on the his head and said, "In the name of God, you are forgiven." That seemed like a nice gesture at the time. The pastor almost immediately began to cry in great, wailing sobs. When the tears no longer came, he said to the one who had offered him the word of forgiveness, "Thank you, and thank God for you."

Most of us can find it in our hearts from time to time to offer forgiveness to someone else for any one of many wrongs, either perceived or real. However, when it comes to offering forgiveness to ourselves, we struggle mightily. Human beings, generally speaking, seem to be their own harshest critics; maybe even their own worst enemies. While we deem others worthy of our forgiveness, we cannot find that same worthiness in ourselves.

Daniel pleaded with God to forgive the Jewish folks for God's own sake! That's pretty bold, don't you think? He had the audacity to suggest to God that God might feel better after offering the people forgiveness. I'm guessing he was relating his own experiences of forgiving and being forgiven; most particularly those times when he had been able to forgive himself.

Even though it may be very difficult, and feel self-serving, true forgiveness must begin with forgiveness of oneself. Any other forgiveness will be shallow, maybe even false, otherwise.

We Wish You a Merry Epiphany, and a Happy New Lent!

Then, opening their treasure chests, they offered him gifts … (Matthew 2:11)

There are a couple of things that I find interesting about January 6. First of all, it starts a period of a few weeks which separate Christmas (when Christians celebrate and acknowledge the birth of Jesus) and Lent (when Christians begin to think about the death of Jesus). For quite a while, that's about all Epiphany meant to me; a time filler. When I got to the seminary, I was informed that Epiphany is actually a time for Christian believers to focus on the divine incarnational act of God in the person of Jesus. I never did figure out why those seminary folks thought they had to try to impress people by using 50 dollar words to explain 50 cent ideas. What they were trying to say is that God came to earth in Jesus. I don't have a problem with that at all. On the other hand, I don't understand why we make such a fuss about it. There are plenty of places in the Bible where we read that the Spirit of God dwells in each of us. In other words (and I know I'm tiptoeing around blasphemy here) I have a notion that the Creator comes to earth every time a baby is born because that is simply the nature of the Creator. Sadly, there has been much strife and consternation in the church over the centuries because of differences of opinion on this whole incarnation thing.

The other thing about January 6th that jumps out at me is that, according to legend at least, it was about then when those three fellows from wherever they were from off to the east came to town with presents for the baby. We don't read about any presents on the day he was born. Shouldn't we be putting up Epiphany trees around the first of the year? Shouldn't we be singing Epiphany carols? Shouldn't we, like those visitors from the east, mark the occasion by giving one another Epiphany presents? What about all those after-Epiphany sales?

I think we've got it all wrong! Besides, the most important thing about January 6 is that it is three days before Aunt Esther's birthday.

Don't Tempt Me

He was in the wilderness forty days, being tempted ... (Mark 1:13)

As I ponder Jesus' forty-day wilderness sojourn it is the first day of a new year. The word "new" seems to bring with it a positive connotation, don't you think? New Year, new car, new hair style, new bleach, New Jersey. We like to think about new replacing what is old. The old year, for better or worse, is over; it is in the past. Can't you just smell that new car smell? 'Man, you need a new hair style. Anything would be better than that pink, orange, and green coiffure you have working right now." "Why, Martha, my clothes are so much brighter and cleaner since I switched to that new bleach." I don't know much about Old Jersey, so I can't talk about that, but I hope you get the point.

The interesting thing is that beginning or acquiring something new can bring along a very real set of temptations as well. New years bring along all kinds of possibilities for being faced with and maybe giving into one kind of temptation or another. New cars bring the temptation to raise our noses just a little bit higher in the air as we drive by our friends who are still puttering around in their old jalopies. The new hairstyle might be even more outlandish and strange than the current one. Too much new bleach will eat holes in your clothes. And, of course, New Jersey has Boardwalk and Park Place.

Mark tells us that, right after he was baptized into a new phase of his life and work, Jesus was immediately tempted for forty straight days. The thing is Mark says he was able to resist the temptations and set a standard none of us can copy. But then, we don't need to. It's enough that he proved that it can be done. Fortunately, God's grace picks up the slack for us.

O God, Save Me from the Savers

"Then who can be saved?" (Mark 10:26)

Ever since Mother and I started going to the Second Salem Baptist Church back in the late 17th century, I've heard well-meaning people talking about being "saved." Starting there at old Second Salem, I've always been curious as to what that meant. I want to know just what it is we're supposed to be saved *from*. Or, could it possibly be that we're supposed to be saved *for* something? On the third hand, might it be that we are supposed to be saved *because of* something, or *in spite of* something? Such a seemingly simple concept fills me with so many questions that I'm not sure which one to ask first.

I can tell you this much; nearly everyone I've ever heard offer a thought on the subject is pretty well certain what ever it means, getting this business of "being saved" done requires some considerable effort on the part of the savee. One response I've received when making an inquiry is that I have to get down on my knees and beg God Almighty to have mercy on my worthless soul so that I might have an outside chance of being saved *from* the eternal fire and damnation of hell itself. The main problem I have with this particular explanation, descriptive and entertaining though it is, is that many who adhere to this particular eschatological worldview reserve the aforementioned consequences for other professing persons of faith whose profession is not of the same ilk as those suggesting the burning and damning.

I've also been told that I need to get myself saved *for* a crown and a mansion in a gold-gilded eternity that some view as heaven. This requires that I somehow prove myself worthy of such eternal bliss. The problem I have with this explanation is that I have no use for a crown, I don't want to have to be bothered with keeping a mansion clean, and gold is such a soft metal that I wouldn't think an eternity made of the stuff would last very long.

"Then who can be saved?" Jesus answered the question 2000 years ago, and apparently not too many people were paying attention. He said, "For mortals it is impossible, but not for God; for God all things are possible." This leads me to believe that all those good church-going believers who tell me I've got work to do don't read the red words in their Bibles, and so they send folks out on a fool's errand. Somehow, we're supposed to get this saving business done by main strength and awkwardness when Jesus already said it's impossible.

Since it is apparently possible for God, though; I'm adding "being saved" to my list of things I need to talk with God about first eternal chance I get. I think God has some explaining to do.

Whatever!

In a certain city there was a judge who neither feared God nor had respect for people ... There was a widow who kept coming to him saying, "Grant me justice against my opponent." For a time he refused; but later he said to himself, "Though I have no fear of God and no respect for anyone, yet because this widow keeps bothering me, I will grant her justice." (Luke 18:2-5)

I know I'm in fairly serious trouble whenever my teenaged daughter comes to me wearing her puppy dog eyes and calls me "Daddy." These are two absolutely reliable indicators that she is about to make a request the nature of which will, in her mind, most likely elicit a negative response from me. When this is the case, she does the best she can to soften me up and make me more amenable. Depending on the request and the amount of money it is likely to cost me; my response may very well *be* negative. At that point, my daughter is much like someone who has applied for Social Security benefits the first time. "No" is the only possible answer; that's just the way it's done, and she accepts that. She generally makes reapplication almost immediately. The eyes may still be in place, but the voice may harden ever so imperceptibly as she now implores, "Why, Dad?" When she was younger, a simple "because I said so" was usually sufficient to buy me some time. She is astute enough now to see through that ruse more often than not. So, I lay out my reasons one by one; point by point. This will cause one of two things to happen. She will either figure that this is an argument she can win or, if victory is in doubt, she will take her plea to her mother in hopes of a more favorable response. This is not a problem unless her mother forgets to ask first what my response was to the original request. If that happens, my young offspring will often return with a smug expression of self-satisfaction and state, "It's alright with Mom."

If I'm feeling particularly energetic, I may suggest that we have a three-way conference after which Mom often says, "Why didn't you tell me what your Dad said?" Under that circumstance, there is still a miniscule chance that the outcome will be favorable for me. If, however, it's late in the day, I'm tired, and the old bones are creaking, "It's alright with Mom" might prompt me to respond as did the unjust judge Jesus talks about as I say, "Whatever."

Of course, the point Jesus makes is that, if an unjust judge or a crotchety old Dad can relent in a just manner, how much more so can we expect God to be just? Further, if God acts justly, how can we who claim to be devotees respond unjustly? Why, that's so incongruent as to be ludicrous.

The Quality of Eternity

"... this is eternal life, that (all people) may know You, the one true God."
(John 17:3)

Today, our discussion group (not a Sunday school class, a discussion group) was talking about the thoughts of the author of a book we have been reading. In the book, the author insists that true believers should not be overly concerned about our life in the present because this is just a test run for something else God has in mind. In fact, the author goes to great length in stating the case that eternity should be our focus. We sat there staring at one another for a minute and then one of the ladies exclaimed, "That's just not right!" She went on to state that, of course, some sort of everlasting relationship with God was her goal, but the life she is living now is the life God has given her for the present, and she feels she owes it to God make the most of it while she's living it.

John makes his case several times that, as a theological concept, eternal life is not to be defined as where we go and what we do after we die. For John, the term "eternal life" describes a quality of life that people of faith can achieve in their relationship with God. Further, John doesn't think of the "sweet by and by" when he's talking about eternal life. It's a here and now proposition. So it doesn't surprise me that in his rendition of that most poignant of discussions with God, John has Jesus define eternal life as people knowing God.

I have to be honest with you; I don't have time to think much about the hereafter, or the hereunder, or the here wherever. God has given me so much to try to do while I'm enjoying my eternal life right now that I'm just going to have to trust that whatever happens after this body dies will be something agreeable to me.

God or Religion?

When Peter went up to Jerusalem, the circumcised believers criticized him, saying, "Why did you go to uncircumcised (people) and eat with them?" Then Peter explained it to them, step by step ... When they heard this, they were silenced. And they praised God, saying, "Then God has given even to the Gentiles the repentance that leads to life." (Acts 11:2-4, 18)

It can be a very disconcerting thing when we find that our religion, upon which so many base so much, is standing in the way of our faith. The two are supposed to compliment one another, are they not? As Peter discovered, religion often harbors and even propagates human biases and bigotries. However, true faith cannot be confined by human foibles. Sometimes in our journey, we are forced to choose.

Peter was, by all accounts, a pretty good Jew. He remembered the Sabbath, to keep it holy. Until recently, he had never eaten anything not entirely kosher. He, along with many of the original disciples, had maintained their adherence to Jewish custom, practice, and rule even after coming under the sway of Jesus. Then, he went to Caesarea at the invitation of a Roman soldier named Cornelius. This was a trip that Peter had no inclination to make. Cornelius had to be a Gentile, most everyone Peter would meet if he went would be a Gentile, and mingling with Gentiles just wasn't done. But then, Peter had a dream. In the dream, he was shown every non-kosher food source known to exist and encouraged by a voice to eat. His religion came into direct conflict with his faith when he was told to do what his religion insisted was wrong. When he made protest the voice said, "God made it; therefore it is clean. Now, eat!" Just as he awoke from this nightmare, there came a knock at his door. It was the men Cornelius had sent to fetch Peter. As soon as Peter laid eyes on them he knew going with them was the right thing to do.

What to do? God or religion; religion or God? Uh ... I think I'll take God.

Regular or Extra Crispy?

Certain individuals came down from Judea and were teaching ..., "Unless you are circumcised according to the custom of Moses, you cannot be saved." And ... Paul and Barnabas had no small dissension and debate with them. (Acts 15:1-2)

The debate just goes on and on; regular or extra crispy, great taste or less filling, thin crust or hand-tossed, circumcised or uncircumcised. In every case it is, or should be, a matter of personal preference. And besides that, in every case the debate boils down to things external which have little to do with what's on the inside. Peel away the regular or extra crispy coating and you still have chicken inside. Whether it tastes great or doesn't fill you up as much, it's still beer. No matter what kind of crust you have, a pizza still has some sort of tomato-based sauce, some cheese, and God only knows what else piled on top.

As far as I'm concerned, it is the same with circumcised or uncircumcised. In this regard, I am in agreement with Peter, and James, and Paul, and Barnabas and a few other notable early disciples of Jesus. They correctly felt that the commitment of one's heart is not related to the ceremonial mutilation of one's body. On the other hand, Luke tells us that there some disciples who belonged to "a sect of the Pharisees," who were of quite a different opinion. They took the position that you can't have Jesus if you don't take Moses. This raises a concern for me on two levels. First of all, how in the world did Pharisees infiltrate the community of believers? That's just scary, don't you think? Also, what does the mutilation of one's body have to do with the content of one's heart? I know I've talked about this before, but it's a point that cannot be overemphasized. Jesus was all about teaching people that things external are of little consequence. As the movement began to grow, influential leaders such as Peter and Paul came to realize just how radical and yet simple the teaching of Jesus really was. As this realization crystallized for them, they saw the implication and began looking for opportunities to share their amazing story beyond the parameters of their ancestral religion. In so doing, they didn't inquire as to the physical characteristics of those with whom they shared. As they went about their business there was backlash. It is that backlash that comes front and center in this part of the story of the Acts of the Apostles. The same thing happened when Larry Doby and Jackie Robinson walked onto major league baseball fields for the first time. The same thing happened when Sandra Day O'Connor was seated on the Supreme Court bench.

Doing what is right often brings with it considerable controversy if the status quo is very strongly entrenched in the tradition of what's not.

The Facts Confuse Me

"Let it be made known then that this salvation of God has been sent to the Gentiles, they will listen." (Acts 28:28)

There is something about the nature of the human animal that just fascinates the living daylights out of me. Why is it, do you suppose, that so many folks believe what they believe so strongly that they refuse to be bothered by the truth? I'm sure you know what I mean: "My dear Captain Columbus, what is this foolishness you speak? Everyone knows that the world is flat." People have an aversion to anything that might challenge what they believe to be true.

Such was Paul's experience. He found himself in Rome the not entirely willing guest of the Emperor. He figured since he was there he might as well do a little work for the cause. He summoned a few of his fellow Jews who were living in Rome for a little powwow to pass the time away. The city of Rome is far enough away from Israel that word of a renegade Jew named Jesus and the trouble he had stirred up had not made its way into the synagogue newsletter in Rome yet. Paul decides to share a bit of what he has come to know as true. Luke says that a few of the local Jews understand what Paul said and accepts its truth for themselves. But then there are some who just don't want to be bothered with the facts. This reality evokes Paul's statement quoted at the beginning of this entry. "Alrighty, then," says Paul. "If those of you who are of the same heritage as Jesus don't want to hear the truth, there are people who do." With that, we're told that he spent the next two years in Rome telling the story to anybody and everybody whose attention he could attract.

I guess there will simply always be those people for whom the facts are irrelevant if the facts are in disagreement with what they believe to be true. I don't understand it, but there you have it.

The Importance of Budget Billing

"I am debtor both to Greeks and to barbarians, both to the wise and the foolish ..." (Romans 1:14)

I don't like being in debt. My daddy told me that a good way to live was to never owe anybody anything. So, the fact that I send a goodly portion of my income every month to make a house payment and a car payment does not rub me in a particularly good way.

I am even more averse to being in debt to another human being because of some favor, either real or perceived, that he or she has done on my behalf. I am very inclined to give of myself for other people, and I do not expect nor do I desire anything in return. Turn the tables, though, and I can not rest until I have somehow satisfied my need to repay whatever debt I feel I have incurred.

Lucky for me, Paul was talking about a different concept altogether here in the first part of his letter to the "believers" in Rome. I read somewhere one time that when Paul talks about "Greeks" and "barbarians" he actually means "those who have class" and "those who are crass." Also, "the wise" actually means "the wise," and "the foolish" actually means "the foolish." The bottom line, though, is that Paul has devoted his time and energy to telling people who aren't Jews about Jesus. Deep stuff, this!

What do you suppose Paul meant when he said he was "debtor" to those who have class, those who are crass, those who are wise, and those who are foolish? Paul was saying that he understands it to be his mission, his call, his destiny, his purpose to talk about Jesus to those folks. He knew that there were others who were laboring among the Jewish folk; that task was well in hand. Therefore, Paul has figured out that he is supposed to labor among everyone else. No small task, I think. In fact it is such a monumental task that Paul feels he owes it to high class/ low class, wise/foolish Gentiles to tell them the story.

If I understand this correctly, by extension I am debtor to any who happen to read these musings. Oh me, oh my; I'm going to have to get on a budget billing plan to pay this off.

When the Spirit Sighs

"The Spirit helps us ... for we do not know how to pray as we ought, but that very Spirit intercedes for us with sighs too deep for words. And God, who searches the heart, knows the mind of the Spirit." (Romans 8:26)

The pager started its incessant beeping. I looked at my watch—3:00 a.m. While I was still clearing the cobwebs from my mind the voice came over the intercom saying, "Code Blue in the Emergency Room. All designated personnel report immediately." I was there because I was spending my Mondays working as a volunteer chaplain at Mercy Medical Center in Des Moines, Iowa. As such, I was one of the "designated personnel."

I made my way to the emergency room and was directed to a cubicle where a man sat sobbing uncontrollably. "Why was it her and not me? Why was it her and not me?" He repeated his question over and over again. An emergency room nurse tapped me just as I was about to enter the cubicle with the man and told me that he and his wife had been traveling home from a party and were hit broadside by a car driven by a man who was under the influence of at least one and possibly more substances. The car driven by the man who was DUI hit the car containing the couple on the passenger's side at a fairly high rate of speed. The woman was killed instantly; the man was not injured.

I had no idea what to say. All my store-bought indoctrination and I had no idea what to say. So ... I didn't say anything. Instead, I sat down by the man and held him while he sobbed. When he had calmed a bit, I made my only statement of the encounter. I said, "I don't have any magic words for you, but, God, this sucks!" "Yeah, it does!" he responded. We sat in silence for a moment longer and the nurse came and asked the man to meet with the coroner. As he left, I muttered, "I'm really sorry." Reflecting on the experience, all I could think about was how totally ineffective and unhelpful I had been.

The next Monday, the head of the Chaplaincy Department handed me an envelope. It contained a card from the man with whom I sat the previous week. In it he had written, "Thank you, from the bottom of my heart. When the nurse told me a chaplain was coming I was afraid you would tell me some "God" stuff to try to make me feel better. Instead, you sat there and hurt with me. God spoke louder to me in the silence of our time together than you could ever have done with your words."

I didn't have any words to say. The Spirit sighed instead.

Separation

"I am convinced that ... nothing in all creation will be able to separate us from the love of God ..." (Romans 8:38-39)

Have you ever had the experience of getting separated? One time, I and some other folks took a group of young people on an outing to a town about thirty miles from where we lived. We all had a great time during the day. When it came time to head home, I had everybody count heads (and the bodies attached to them) and we loaded the cars and off we went. About ten miles down the road one of the cars came roaring up beside me and the woman driving motioned for me to pull over. She came running frantically to my car screaming, "Scott and Kevin aren't here! Scott and Kevin aren't here!" Turns out that she thought Scott and Kevin were in another car and the driver of the other car thought Scott and Kevin were with her. I was a bit perplexed since it would be me looking into the eyes of Scott's dad and Kevin's mom saying, "We got separated and we lost them."

I decided that we had to go back and look for Scott and Kevin. So, we got the horses and wagons turned around and headed back to where we had just come from. When we got there, there was a police car sitting in the parking lot. Scott, Kevin, and a member of the law enforcement community were there. When the boys realized what had happened, they flagged down the policeman and were trying to contact their parents when we arrived. You talk about relief! I felt as though my life had just been handed back to me.

That's all small 'taters compared to what Paul is talking about. His experience has led him to believe that God's love is so vast and all-encompassing that nothing short of the Creator can separate people from the Creator. "Nothing in all creation" Paul says. Not even death. What kind of commitment is it that God is willing to make that is so strong that not even death can get in the way of it?

I highly recommend taking along a checklist and counting every nose yourself if you ever take the young folks on an outing. Or at least have some tin cans and a really long ball of string so you can talk to the folks in the car behind you.

Living Honorably

"… Salvation is nearer to us now than when we became believers; … let us live honorably." (Romans 13:11-12)

I've got one of those annotated bibles. Along left and right margins on each page are short little statements that the editor stuck in there so that we uninformed folks can know what the words really mean. Right along side the verses from which I quoted, it says, "Eschatology and morality are often connected." That clears things right up, doesn't it?

"Eschatology and morality are often connected." When I was receiving my seminary indoctrination, I was told that eschatology was the discipline of studying and considering the end of time. When I asked, "Why don't we just say that," I was emphatically reminded that I was now studying among the theologically elite and should conduct myself accordingly. Any way, as I waded through all that institutional pomposity, I figured out that Paul, and quite a few other folks in the first few decades of the Christian movement, were convinced that they were living at the end of time. As it turns out, they *were* living at the end of *their* time. Nonetheless, they figured that, since it wouldn't be too long before they would get to make the face-to-face acquaintance of God, it would most likely be best if they could offer a good accounting of themselves when the introductions were made. So, Paul puts this little disclaimer in his letter to the community in Rome. Rome, along with Greece, as you may recall had a noticeable reputation for throwing some outrageous parties. Paul is reminding people that they should consider just what it is they would like to visit with God about when the times comes. Thus, in reminding the people to live responsibly and morally, he ties it to their impending eternal future.

Now, it seems to me that even though a couple thousand years have come and gone without the occurrence of the eschatological fulfillment which Paul was expecting, what he said is still true. For every one of us, salvation becomes nearer every day. In other words, the approach of *our* eschatological fulfillment inches ever closer.

I have decided that until I become a part of some eschatological reality, living honorably to the best of my ability might not be a bad idea at all.

Judge Not; Unless, of Course, You Would Care to be Judged

"… Let us (not) pass judgment on one another." (Romans 14:13)

A little over two years ago, something sad happened in our community. We have a big reservoir east of town that the power company built as a cooling pool for the nuclear powered generator it built out there. Somehow or another, on a warm September evening, a car with three little children securely strapped in their car seats rolled down a boat ramp into that lake and the children all drowned. The mother of the children and her gentleman friend were present when this tragedy occurred. Many things about the events of the evening made our enforcers of the law suspicious. After doing a little investigating they placed the mother and her friend under arrest. Next, it was announced that a grand jury would be convened. The responsibility of the grand jury would be to make a determination as to whether or not enough evidence existed to charge mother and friend with murder. As fate would have it, my name was drawn out of the hat to be a member of that grand jury. I rationalized to myself that I would be able to handle the assignment since it would not fall to the grand jury to determine guilt or innocence. All we had to do was say whether or not it appeared that two people could be charged with something.

Once the grand jury was called together, it quickly became apparent that police and lawyers did, in fact, have an expectation that we would be passing a judgment of one kind or another. We were bombarded with facts, and figures, and material witnesses and photographic reenactments. Then, we were presented with what could only be classified as pleading on the part of the officials to let them press charges.

I hope I'm never put in that position again. As near as I can tell, any judging that needs to be done, God will do. Call me a wimp if you want to, but I don't want to be anybody's judge.

Talking About Real Love

"... now faith, hope, and love abide, these three; and the greatest of these is love."

(I Corinthians 13:13)

Today is Valentine's Day. I think I saw more candy and flowers being passed around today than I've ever seen in my life. I guess it's too bad that the fragrance of flowers makes it hard for me to breathe and candy gives me a belly ache. Those two things sure seem to be what defines this day in our culture.

It can be no coincidence that the American Bible Society chose I Corinthians 13 as the Bible reading for the day. Love, love, and more love. I've talked before about what I think of most definitions and/or expressions of love. The thing is Paul actually makes a pretty good point here. The folks in the church at Corinth set a great store in having some noticeable "spiritual" gift that made them unique from each other. There were those who loved to brag because they had spoken in some other language that nobody understood, including the person speaking it. They figured that made them more Christian than anybody else. Others of them had come to the conclusion that they were seers who could predict tomorrow. Of course, that made them more Christian than anybody else. Still others of them told anybody who would listen that they gave their whole paycheck to the soup kitchen and volunteered there eight days each week. The fact that they were so giving and self-sacrificing obviously made them more Christian than anybody else. Getting one up on somebody else for God's sake was the name of the game in the Corinthian Christian Circle (CCC).

Paul heard about what was going on there in the CCC and decided that a little lesson in humility might be in order. "So," he said, "you think you're special because you can speak in some foreign language that even you don't understand. I'm not impressed." He went on to say that if folks with that gift felt like they needed to brag about it, then they were missing the point. The only reason that any person is ever given any gift is so that he or she can more fully show God's love for somebody else. "So," said Paul, "you think you're special because you can predict the future. So what?" He was making the point that the future doesn't matter much if we're so concerned with it that we aren't loving folks today. "So," Paul stated, "You want people to notice that you give all your money and your time to the soup kitchen. Big deal. If you were doing it because of your love for other people, it wouldn't matter if anybody knew about it or not."

He finishes up by saying that faith is a fine thing, everybody ought to have some. Hope, that's good, too. It gives us a reason to get up in the morning. But love; now that's really something. It would be pretty hard to keep the faith or have any hope if there was no sense of the reality of love. That's not just a spiritual reality; that's a psychological reality as well.

Love, real love. It's not that mushy-gushy stuff that people want to talk about, especially on Valentine's Day. Real love is the ability to have positive regard for other human beings, simply because they, too, are human beings. Real love is that recognition that every person was created by God and is, therefore, inherently worthy of positive regard. Some of them may not realize it or act like it, but that doesn't change it.

How Do You Say "Cement?"

"I urge Euodia and Syntyche to be of the same mind in the Lord, for (these women) have struggled beside me in the work of the gospel." (Phillipians 4:2-3)

One time when I was six or seven, our family went vacationing in the northern part of the Lower Peninsula of Michigan. My great-uncle owned a cottage on a lake there; it was a beautiful place. Along about the second day, I was playing in the sand at the beach. Another boy about my age came up and we began to build things together in the sand. It had rained a little not long before, the sun had come out, and some of the sand was a little crusty. I said, "Man, this stuff is like CE-ment." "You said that wrong," opined my companion, "It's ce-MENT." "CE-ment," I retorted. "ce-MENT," he insisted. The next thing you know, we were engaged in a desperate, life-and-death struggle. We put sand in each other's underwear, and tried to get some in each other's mouths, eyes, ears, and nose. Finally, an adult of some vintage overheard the sounds of our raging battle. Once we were separated, the adult asked us, "What was *that* all about?" The other boy and I pointed at one another and simultaneously declared, "He says CE-ment/ce-MENT wrong!" We had very different opinions about the same thing, and those opinions were important enough to us to lead us into hand-to-hand combat.

I've seen the same thing happen quite often in church meetings. Should worship take place at 9:15 or 10:30? Should the offering be before or after the sermon? Should we send five young people to camp or put carpet on the bathroom floor? On and on it goes. It was apparently happening in the Philippian church, too. Euodia and Syntyche were, it seems, two of the more influential persons in the congregation. It should come as no surprise that they were women. I have never, ever been in a church yet, regardless of denomination, doctrine, dogma, or theology, the backbone of which was not the women. Get used to it, men. You may refuse to ordain them due to some misguided and archaic interpretation of a verse in the Bible, you might attempt to exclude them from official positions of leadership. Be not deceived, however. Women form the backbone of every congregation with which I have ever had contact. And I say thank God this is so!

Oops, I started preaching there, didn't I? Anyway, back to Philippi. Euodia and Syntyche were on the outs about something down at the church house. Now, people will have disagreements from time to time. That's just the nature of people. However, Paul recognized how destructive disagreement can be if it occurs between those viewed as the leadership. This was particularly true in the beginning as these congregations were trying to survive and grow in what was usually a hostile environment. What the people needed to see was unity of leadership, not division. Paul knew it, and he called the ladies on it.

It is the same today. Those in positions of leadership may not agree on some things; that will happen. They need, however, to keep the disagreement from public view. Hopefully they are in positions of leadership because they can lead. A good leader knows that public disagreement can cause dissension, and keeps it in its proper place. When we are about doing God's business, that's how it must be.

Faith as Algebra

"We have heard of your faith … and of the love that you have for all the saints … because of the hope laid up for you in heaven." (Colossians 1:4-5)

Paul seems to hold the folks at Colossae in fairly high regard. He is not at all sparing in his praise of and commendation for them. He starts his letter to them with his own version of the theological trinity: faith, love, hope. If I'm not mistaken, those themes show up in other places in his writings.

Here, though, he lays it out just a bit differently. First, he mentions the faith that the Colossians are developing as they move along in their spiritual journey. Next he notes that this faith is moving them to love "all the saints." He caps it off by indicating that their faith and love are possible because they have chosen to hope in the promise of God's eternity.

It's all quite logical, really; even algebraic. Paul uses a formula here that makes perfect sense. It looks something like this: $(f + l)^h = e$. Would you believe I failed Advanced Algebra in high school and came up with that, anyway? But, that's what it is: Faith plus Love multiplied by the power of Hope equals Eternity.

As I have mentioned many times before, people often seem to try valiantly to make things harder than they need to be. They just can't get past their ruggedly individualistic notions of needing to achieve everything (including things spiritual) through main strength and awkwardness. I wish they could understand that they really don't have to work that hard at it since to do so is unnecessary and will ultimately prove to be fruitless. They employ their own algebraic formula which looks like this: $3m^w = e$; me times myself times I to the power of my work equals eternity. The problem with this formula is that it can never produce a workable version of "e". In fact, in this equation, "e" stands for exhaustion of the spiritual variety which, I believe, is not a necessarily good thing.

I Forgive Me

"Bear with one another, ... and forgive one another." (Colossians 3:13)

A friend of mind has dedicated a good part of her life to working with persons addicted to chemical substances in their struggle to be free. She tells some remarkable stories of the odds that people have overcome on the road to recovery.

Recently she shared about a friend of hers who was finally successful in the struggle in an ultimate sort of way. Her friend struggled for most of his life with his addiction, attempting many times to break free. At one time, she says that he was sober for three weeks. That may sound feeble to many, but for one so completely under the control of foreign substances, those three weeks were a major victory. Not long ago, though, he broke free in what may have been the only way he saw left to him. He gained access to and consumed sufficient quantities of substances that he overdosed and died.

As my friend told this story, she admitted that she felt guilt along with her sorrow because she hadn't been able to bring this man through to recovery. She felt that there should have been something else she could have done. As I listened to her, it dawned on me that she was expressing a deep need. She needed to forgive herself.

Paul suggests to the folks in the region of Colassae that one of the best ways for them to live out their faith is to "bear with one another ... and forgive one another." I would submit that this admonition also includes forgiving oneself. My experience has been that most people can forgive someone else for a transgression, either real or perceived. My experience has also been that those same people have one dickens of a time when it comes to forgiving themselves. Human beings seem to be far harsher with, more critical of, and less forgiving of themselves than God or their fellow human beings would ever be.

Sometimes, we need to have the courage to look into a mirror and say to the person looking back at us, "I forgive you."

What in the World is Faith, Anyway?

*"Brothers and sisters, partners in a heavenly calling, consider that Jesus ...
was faithful to the one who appointed him." (Hebrews 3:1-2)*

Over the last 30 years, I have probably asked at least seventy-five men and an equal number of women if they will commit to being faithful to one another for the rest of their lives. This question comes somewhere before, "Well, kiss her, for Pete's sake!" In that context what is being asked of these people is whether or not they believe that they can prevent any other person, or thing, or situation from disrupting or interfering with the relationship upon which they are embarking. Thus, in this context, faithful means unwavering.

Out West, there's that world famous geyser; let's see, what is it called? Oh, now I remember: Old Faithful. This geyser is so named because its eruptions are chronologically predictable. Thus, in this context, faithful means unchanging.

At church, people talk all the time about being faithful. The kicker is that they are talking about being faithful to someone or something the existence of whom or which they cannot prove. Thus, in this context, faithful means trusting that something unprovable may be, nonetheless, true.

One of the first songs I learned to play on the 12-string guitar was called "As Tears Go By." I learned the song from a recording by Maryanne Faithful. In this context, I have absolutely no idea what faithful means.

In the statement above written by the author of the Book of the Hebrews, it says that, "Jesus was faithful to the one who appointed him." In this context, faithful means something very different than what I have heretofore described. In this context, faithful means that Jesus did what he believed would be pleasing to God. His actions reflected his relationship with God. His lifestyle was a manifestation of his spiritual nature. In other words, he was who he felt God expected him to be. Thus, in this context, faithful means loyal.

Summing this up, it seems to me that to be faithful is to be unwaveringly, predictably, loyally trusting that something unprovable may be, nonetheless, true. I do believe that the two most compelling aspects of this description are loyalty and trust. It seems to me that without loyalty and trust, being faithful is simply not possible. In fact, when Maryanne Faithful sang "As Tears Go By," she was singing about having faithfulness destroyed by lack of loyalty and trust.

Ms. Faithful faithfully shared an eternal truism about being faithful. To be faithful simply is not possible without loyalty and trust.

Remember the Sabbath

"A sabbath rest still remains for the people of God ... Let us therefore make every effort to enter into that rest." (Hebrews 4:9, 11)

I once read that the literal meaning of the word "sabbath" is to rest from labor. The interesting thing is that this definition does not mention Saturday or Sunday or any other day ending with the letter "y." Sabbath means to take a break from work; to take a day off. A very simple concept, really. In fact, taking a day off is so important that it made it into the top ten commandments of all time. And so what have religious people done with it? Some have made hundreds of minutely defined laws intended to inform others as to what they can and cannot do on their day off. Would you believe that there have been people who were killed because they did something on their day off that violated someone else's religious sensibility?

The whole thing is arbitrary, anyway. As I inferred just now, many people tie their day off intimately to whatever their religion dictates. They take this to such an extreme that they even capitalize the first letter of the word "sabbath" no matter where it appears in a sentence. Once that is accomplished, then they buy into the propaganda that they can only take their day off on a certain day, like Saturday or Sunday. I've always been curious as to who decided that, anyway.

Many Christian folk adhere to a well-established double standard regarding the sabbath. Of course, most of them insist that people's day off has to be Sunday, in honor of the notion that Jesus reportedly decided on Sunday not to be dead anymore. The majority of these folk are quite staunch in their conviction that you shouldn't work on Sunday unless your ox is in the ditch, to misquote a statement from the Hebrew Scriptures. Even so, it would be unheard of for a Christian who makes her or his living in the service of the religion to make Sunday his or her sabbath. Instead, Sunday becomes the second busiest work day of the week for these professional Christians; second only to Wednesday since Wednesday night is church meeting night. The sabbath for these folk is supposed to be on a day in which their services aren't required by the rest of the Christians who write the paycheck. Am I the only one who sees incongruity here? I'm not being critical, really I'm not; just observant. I can tell you this: when I got to the place where I needed six sabbaths to recover from the Sabbath, I knew it was time to do something different.

Thus, I no longer derive my living from a religious institution. I derive my living doing things that actually allow me to have a sabbath. I still serve as a pastor on Sunday because I choose to; not because my livelihood depends on it. That is how it should be for everybody.

Who Spiked the Punch?

"… Do not be carried away by all kinds of strange teachings; for it is well for the heart to be strengthened by grace, not by regulations … which have not benefited those who observe them." (Hebrews 13:9)

I was involved with the Methodist/United Methodist Church during my formative years. So was an idealistic young preacher named Jones; James Jones. Somewhere along the way, Jim (as he was called) saw his idealism transform into fanaticism to such a degree that those good Methodists saw fit to uninvite him from being a member of their professional ministerial leadership.

A few years later, Jim resurfaced in San Francisco where he started up his own little meeting that came to be called The People's Temple. After a while, these folks wore out their welcome in that fair California metropolis and moved to the jungles of South America. Is any of this starting to sound familiar yet? There came that fateful day when the communion juice was spiked with poison and all 900 and however many willingly partook, lay down, and died. As the writer of Hebrews puts it, they had been "carried away by all kinds of strange teachings."

Most of the major Christian denominations have some sort of book or document which lays out the regulations that must be followed in order to be an acceptable member of the organization. These documents range from relatively small pamphlets to tomes hundreds of pages long. Now, remember I specifically mentioned that I am referring to Christian denominations. In other words, each of them supposedly exists for the same purpose—to extol the virtues of a relationship with God that includes Jesus. I find it interesting that every one of the books of rules to which someone is expected to adhere places different restrictions on being one of the faithful. Some have rules that say you aren't "Christian" if you haven't had your whole body dunked in some body of water or another. Some say that if you build a building in which to worship, it doesn't belong to you; it belongs to some committee in an office miles away, most of whom don't know who you are or where your building is. Some insist that God is gender-specific when calling people to a life of service. I could go on and on, but are you getting my point?

There doesn't seem to be much room for "the heart to be strengthened by grace." Instead, in true pharisaic fashion, people who choose to be a part of a denomination find themselves bound to "regulations ... which have not benefited those who observe them."

I think maybe the people in control of these denominational institutions have chosen to remove Hebrews 13:9 from their bibles.

Riddle's Grace

"How does God's love abide in anyone who has the world's goods and sees a brother or sister in need and yet refuses help?" (I John 3:17)

In the preface for this collection of essays, I mentioned that my parents live back in a holler down below Riddle Ridge in the southern Indiana hills. Up on top of Riddle Ridge sits a little white one-room church house. The sign outside says that it is the Riddle United Methodist Church. I don't suppose there are very many folks living on or around the Ridge that have much knowledge about the United Methodist business. That little white building up on top of the knob is simply the Riddle church. It's been there since the late 1800s, serving as the spiritual beacon for the surrounding countryside. The pastor is a beautiful woman in her 70s who lives right down the road. She is what the United Methodists call a lay speaker. She hasn't been indoctrinated by a seminary education; she hasn't been "ordained" by the institution. She just has a real love for God, and her greatest joy is talking about it. On any given Sunday, the congregation who gathers with her there will range from 5 to 10 faithful souls.

I tell you about this remarkable little community of faith because they have asked themselves the question posed in I John 3:17 and decided that God's love dictates that they *must* help brothers and sisters in need. For example, you may remember when Hurricane Katrina devastated the gulf coast of our country. During worship the next Sunday, the Riddle folks were talking about it and decided that they ought to stop talking and start doing. So, the word went out all across the Ridge and the next Sunday there was $1,000.00 in the plate to be sent to folks whose lives and possessions had been damaged or destroyed by the hurricane. Now, that might not sound like a big deal, but let me tell you something. Riddle Ridge is in Crawford County, Indiana which is one of the poorest counties in that state. Nonetheless, those folks know that when someone somewhere is worse off than them, they need to do something about it.

I should also mention that the Riddle Ridge community is not driven by any notions of having to work for their salvation. They respond as they do to the needs of others because of how gracious they figure God has been to them. They are living proof that grace begets grace. That's how it's supposed to work.

God Believes in You ... and You
... and You

"In this is love, not that we loved God but that (God) loved us ..." (I John 4:10)

One of my very favorite stories has Archbishop Desmond Tutu as one of the two principle participants. I heard the story so long ago that I have no recollection where I heard it or from whom, thus I must say before I proceed, "To whoever shared this wonderful story with me, thank you and please consider this as giving you proper credit."

As the tale begins, Bishop Tutu has been speaking or preaching in some public venue or another. Upon finishing his discourse, he is personally greeting many of those who have been in attendance. After a time, a gentleman approaches and says, "Bishop Tutu, I found what you had to say most interesting. I want you to know, however, that I am an atheist and I do not believe in your God." To which Bishop Tutu calmly replies (and I'm paraphrasing), "That you do not believe in my God is inconsequential because, you see, my God believes in you."

My God believes in you. "In this is love, not that we loved God but that (God) loves us." Two phrases spoken thousands of years apart, yet conveying the same message. God is not bound by what we humans believe about God. God does not love only those who we deem worthy of God's love. God does not find acceptable only those who subscribe to our dogma or our doctrine or our discipline. Any attempt made by any person or institution to define God's parameters according to a particular world view (or *other* worldly view, as the case may be) is ultimately doomed to failure.

What ever awaits us on the other side of death is, I think, going to come as a shock to many, many people. This will especially be the case, I suspect, for those who lived their lives insisting that they knew God's nature and had the *only* true knowledge of that nature. They're going to be bumping into all kinds of folks who they tried desperately to condemn to a fate which God did not intend.

Who is The Temple?

"I saw no temple in the city, for its temple is the Lord God the Almighty."
(Revelation 21:22)

I teach a course in world religions for an online, virtual institution of higher learning. One of the fascinating things about comparing and contrasting various religious traditions is considering the places where adherents, practitioners, or whatever they might be called gather to worship. On the one hand, Jews and Christians and Muslims have built some of the most marvelously grand architectural wonders known to human kind. It would really difficult to miss one of these temples; they are impressive!

On the other hand, a faithful Hindu or Buddhist may have some sort of shrine set up on a stand in their bedroom where they do their worshipping in solitude. If you were unacquainted with these worship practices, you may never see the temple; its existence would simply be unknown to all but the one who worships there. Are the grand edifices better places to worship than the bedroom shrine? I'm guessing most likely not. Each serves its intended purpose and meets the need of those worshipping.

Of course, John was trying to tell his friends and neighbors and loved ones that Rome would not be in power forever. Jerusalem would not be an occupied city indefinitely. He used apocalyptic as his literary form and spoke in terms of dreams and visions and signs and symbols because he knew that his intended audience would be able to appropriately interpret his words while most Romans would not. As a means of offering hope to a people oppressed (doesn't this sound like Second and Third Isaiah as they talked to people who had lived through the reality of Babylonian oppression?), John talks about a day when the present Jerusalem would be replaced by a new and improved model. As part of the description, John states what I quoted above; "I saw no temple." No temple; no First United Baptist Church of the Presbyterian Methodist Persuasion; no synagogue; no mosque. That just doesn't sound right, does it? I mean, really; we have to have a place to go to meeting, don't we?

Well; no, not really. John says something really interesting, "the temple is the Lord God the Almighty." I kind of have an idea that John was reassuring the people that, even though the temple might be utterly destroyed, still God will be God and God will continue to be worthy of worship. I really and truly believe that there is a strong prophetic message here for people who want their church house to be bigger and fancier with more bells and whistles than the folks down the street. Their priorities are in the wrong place. The building is not the temple; God is the temple.

Take that money in the building fund and feed some hungry people with it. No matter how much of it you spend on a building, God won't be impressed.

How About Worshipping God for a Change?

I, John, am the one who heard and saw these things. And when I heard and saw them, I fell down to worship at the feet of the angel who showed them to me, but the angel said to me, "You must not do that! I am a fellow servant with you and the prophets. Worship God!" (Revelation 22:8-9)

John of Patmos writes these words near the end of his apocalyptic drama, and they are the most important words in the whole parable. He tried to make a mistake that many people make. What is that mistake? That mistake is worshipping the messenger rather than the author of the message. It happens all the time. I know people who will actually move with a particular pastor to whatever community he or she is called to so that they can continue to bask in her or his glow! They are worshipping the messenger.

There are people who speak of Billy Graham only in the most hushed and reverent tones. They are worshipping the messenger. There are those who get sucked into the hucksterish gibberish of television evangelist after television evangelist and send these charlatans their money, even money they cannot afford to send. They are worshipping the messenger. Sometimes I will hear some of my Protestant sisters and brothers speaking derisively about my Catholic sisters and brothers because they have icons of beloved saints in their church. Yet many of those Protestant sisters and brothers make a great ritual of having some huge, old Bible carried into and out of the sanctuary as part of their ongoing worship experience. Sounds like another icon to me. In this case, it seems that people may be worshipping, not so much the messenger, but a copy of the message.

Most insidious of all are those who insist on worshipping the original messenger. Please help me understand why someone would make the dread mistake of worshipping Jesus? That is the highest form of idolatry and is the very kind of foolishness he tried so hard to eradicate. Even at his most spiritual moments, he never drew the attention to himself. Remember all those times when he talked in terms of, "Not me, but the One who sent me"?

212

As I said, John almost fell into the same trap. According to the way he tells it the story was shared with him by an angel. For those who believe in angels, that would be pretty nifty, don't you think? But, John is so overwhelmed by the story that he forgets himself for a minute, and starts to worship the angel. The angel immediately stops him. "Not in this lifetime, or the lifetime to come!" the angel warns. "I'm a working stiff just like you," the angel continues. "I was given a job to do, and I've done it."

Why do you suppose John makes a point of including this little exchange in his story? Because he doesn't want other people making the same mistake he almost made. Funny thing is, as I mentioned earlier, people go right ahead and make that mistake anyway. I think they better listen clearly to what that angel says, "Worship God!"

UP TO THE
CHALLENGE?

Uncertain, Impatient Doubt

The word of the Lord came to Abram in a vision. "Do not be afraid, Abram, I am your shield; your reward shall be very great." But Abram said, "'O Lord God, what will You give me, for I continue childless ... You have given me no offspring ... " (Genesis 15:1-3)

After Roxanne and I were married, we lived in a house owned by the churches that she was serving as pastor. It was a nice 3-bedroom ranch with far more room than the two of us needed. As we began to dream in earnest of our future together, one of the unused bedrooms came to be called "Andrew's room." We somehow had come to the mutual idea that we would have a child, it would be a boy, Andrew would be his name, and he would inhabit that unused bedroom.

Three years later, Roxanne graduated from seminary and we prepared to move to Iowa. Andrew's room remained vacant. When we left that house, we left our thoughts of a boy named Andrew there as well.

We lived in Iowa for five years. While there, we lived in a new, very large 3-bedroom home with a full basement and every amenity you could imagine. For five years, two of those three bedrooms remained vacant. At the end of those five years, Roxanne and I had come to the conclusion that we were to remain childless.

When we were both 37 years old, we moved into a five-bedroom home in Illinois where we lived for 3 years. After two of those years had passed and we still had no heir to carry on our family legacies, we decided to adopt a child. Maria came to be our daughter during the third year of our stay there. At the same time that we found that we would be blessed by being her parents, Roxanne became pregnant! Two months after our 40th birthdays, Cristina was born.

I share this story to say that I can empathize with Abram's doubt and uncertainty. Being long past what is considered a "normal" age for producing heirs, both he and I had become skeptical. What Abram and I discovered is that, when it comes to understanding what God might consider "normal," neither of us had a clue.

It's hard to be patient when God simply refuses to act in an efficient and timely manner. Being prideful as I am, it's even more difficult to have to admit that God had things under control the whole time. You'd think that God would figure out that I don't like not being in control.

On the other hand, I'm sure my folly gives God much opportunity for mirth and merriment.

But, I Don't Want To

Moses (said), "But suppose they do not believe me or listen to me" … Moses said to the Lord, "O my Lord, I have never been eloquent, neither in the past nor even now that You have spoken to Your servant; but I am slow of speech and slow of tongue" … (Moses) said, "O my Lord, please send someone else."
(Exodus 4:1, 10, 14)

The last time I was in the cast of a theatrical production was in 1968. The young people of the church I was attending decided to put on a play we had seen at camp the previous summer. One of the other young men played this thug who had a bit of an attitude problem. At one point in the story, he was to pull a knife on another guy. We wanted to be realistic, so somebody (I really don't remember who) brought his dad's skinning knife for use as a prop. That was one really cool knife, let me tell you. I was really fascinated by it and, being the dumb teenager that I was, I picked it up and began to brandish it just a bit. To this day I don't know how it happened, but at some point in my brandishment, Phyllis Irvin backed into that blade. It immediately and seriously sliced her elbow. She screamed and I wanted to crawl into a hole. Sharp knives have made me uncomfortable since that night and I have never again desired to take the stage as an actor in the intervening 39 years.

Someone who could drive took Phyllis home and someone else who could drive took me home. When I got there, I was shaking pretty badly. I told Mother and Dad what had happened and that it was my fault because I was being careless. I then threw myself upon their mercy and pleaded with them to call Phyllis' parents and explain what happened. "No," came the calm, yet definite reply. "This is something you have to do," one or the other of them said. "Is this negotiable?" I desperately asked. "No," came the firm, and definite reply. "This is something you have to do," one or the other of them said. "How about if I wash the dishes for a week, do my own laundry, actually treat my sisters nicely, and do an expose' on the fallacies of metaphysical philosphy" was my last-ditch plea. "No," came the insistent and even more definite reply. "This is something you have to do," one or the other of them said. Making that phone call was one of the hardest things I've ever had to do. I would have gladly exchanged that experience for a solid, accurately placed boot to the rear.

Moses was in the same kind of a fix. God was directing him to do something he absolutely did not want to do. So, he tried every excuse he could think of to talk God out of this obviously misguided plan. God put up with the "But … but … but …" for a while, and then the One, the only, the Almighty had a belly full and basically told Moses, "You're going; I've already decided. Get used to the idea."

I know of a really good Gouda cheese that goes well with the type of whine Moses and I were trying to pour.

This Water Tastes Funny

They went three days in the wilderness and found no water. When they came to Marah (which means "bitterness"), they could not drink the water of Marah because it was bitter. And the people complained against Moses, saying, "What shall we drink?" Moses threw a piece of wood in the water, and the water became sweet. (Exodus 15:22b-25)

Several years ago, Roxanne and I moved to a small town in Illinois where I was to be the United Methodist pastor while she went to school at Garrett-Evangelical Theological Seminary which is part of Northwestern University. After we moved into the house that was being provided for us, I was thirsty. I went to the kitchen sink and ran a glass full of water which it was my intention to drink in its entirety in as short a period of time as possible. In the glass, it looked like water as nearly as I could tell. As I tipped the glass toward my parched, dry mouth, I noticed the faintest hint of a not entirely pleasant aroma. Then, the water entered my mouth and exited my mouth almost simultaneously. Never in my life had I offended my pallet with anything so foul-tasting. It turns out that the folks in the community had forgotten to warn us not to drink their water. During our second year there, the town dug a new well in hopes of lessening significantly the nastiness factor of the water supply. They tapped into the very same vein of water and wound up having two means by which to extract the same awful liquid from its underground repository. I looked everywhere for a sweetwater stick, but I never found one.

It is true that the water those intrepid Israelites came upon at Marah was less than borderline potable. It is true that Moses was able to rectify the situation. What is significant about this episode, however, is the fickle nature of the people. Just three days prior to this, they had marched across the marshy Sea of Reeds to final freedom from Pharaoh ending a period of servitude many hundreds of years old. Now, the first time they are inconvenienced a bit, the Israelites begin their complaints almost immediately.

It seems to be human nature that gratitude be an inconsistent, only-when-we-feel-like-it proposition at best. We are grateful until the next problem comes along and then we are back to whining and complaining again. I have a suspicion that if people could find something for which to be grateful even when things aren't particularly peachy then life, like water, might actually become more potable.

Give Me That Old Time Religion

"Do not remember the former things, or consider the things of old, I am about to do a new thing ..." (Isaiah 43:18-19)

The following statements are ones which, if uttered within my hearing even one more time, will cause me to lose my religion (wait a minute; I'm not religious!):

1. We've always done it that way.

2. I remember when ... (fill in your own ending to this one).

3. Why can't things be like they used to be?

4. But the King Jimmy bible says....

5. Give me that old time religion; it's good enough for me.

I've tried for a number of years now to understand why people are so blasted insistent on living their lives yesterday. Time moves them inexorably forward, but they are always looking back over their shoulder. It's a wonder to me that they aren't constantly running into things and hurting themselves.

Example: There's a little congregation I know of that has an old, rickety, past-its-prime serving table in the fellowship hall. I'd be hesitant to set a balloon bouquet on the thing for fear that it might collapse from the weight. Some of the good reasonable folk in that group came to the conclusion that the table had served admirably ever since it had been donated in 1893, could be honorably retired, and replaced by a newer, more sturdy model. Within a matter of hours it was all over town that the church was going to scrap the table that so-and-so's grandma's uncle's third wife donated in 1893. You never heard such an outcry of protest in your life. Why, that church was just full of ungrateful people; that's what it was. Last I knew the table was still in the fellowship hall.

People need to listen to what Isaiah suggests God is saying. Remember, at the time, the Jews were still captives in Babylon looking forward to going home. Apparently, more than a few of them were getting excited about not only going home, but getting back to the good old days. So, Isaiah had God say to them that they couldn't look forward to what used to be. What used to be was gone, done, over, finished. It might have been good; it might have been bad. Either way, that was then, and this is now. God said that a new thing was in the works; a *new* thing.

God has new things in the works all the time. I bet we miss three-fourths of them because we won't stop wishing for the old things long enough to see what might yet be.

That old table has to go, before somebody gets hurt.

God Likes Me Best

Thus says the Lord to (the) anointed, to Cyrus, "For the sake of My servant Jacob, and Israel My chosen, I call you by your name, … though you do not know Me. I am the Lord, and there is no other, beside me there is no god … "
(Isaiah 45:1, 4-5)

Here we have quite an interesting situation. Second Isaiah is speaking for God again, and God is saying that Cyrus has been chosen to do a good thing for the people of Israel who, as you know, are still being held captive in Babylon. This wouldn't be worthy of mention except for the fact that Cyrus is not next in line to assume the throne of Israel. Cyrus is a Persian warrior who has taken over Babylon and is about to clean house. What's even more interesting is that Cyrus did not worship the God of Israel. Nonetheless, God makes it plain that Cyrus is doing God's bidding according to God's plan.

Now, there are a couple of ways to look at this. First of all, if I was Cyrus, and this kind of talk got out, I would have a ruffled feather or four. I'm one of those people who really doesn't like somebody else doing my thinking for me, making my decisions for me, or using me for devices not of my own creation. This is particularly true if that somebody happens to be one with whom I have no relationship. So, what must Cyrus have been thinking? "Hey, Cyrus, the word on the street is that some pipsqueak prophet from that squirrelly band of people the Babylonians have been keeping as house pets is saying that you are the chosen instrument of their God," says a paid informant. "Oh, really," says Cyrus, "I don't know about that, but I *am* going to send them home."

On the other hand, this story should really just irritate the dickens out of all those Jews and Christians who are insistent on believing that God would never accomplish God's purposes through any other than they, and they alone. I'd love for all of them to read about old Cyrus just so I could see how upset they get.

Now, that's not nice of me, is it? I'm sorry, God.

The fact is the sooner people can once and for all figure out that God created all of us, God loves all of us, and God will use all of us as necessary, the better off we'll all be. It won't happen in my lifetime, and maybe never. Nonetheless, that's how I see it.

Get Together

Thus says the Lord God: "I will take the people of Israel from the nations among which they have gone, … and will bring them to their own land. I will make them one nation in the land … Never again shall they be two nations, and never again shall they be divided into two kingdoms." (Ezekiel 37:21-22)

For nearly a year now, I have been a member of the faculty of a "virtual" university. I teach a course which explores the major religions of the world in an online, computer-driven classroom. Teaching this class has brought into focus some thoughts that have been rolling around in my brain like dice in a cup for the past few years. Of course, I have been very unapologetically clear about my notions considering religion—I don't care much for it. On the other hand, for almost as long as human beings have been conscious enough to realize that they are part of a universe too vast to be an accident, they have been striving to find ways to say "thank you" to whoever designed and built the whole thing. The only fault I find with that is the way in which different groups of people develop the notion that their way of saying "thanks" is better or more spiritual or more holy or more righteous than others. They go so far as to devise rules to dictate the way in which "thanks" may be said, and insist that if these rules aren't followed, then when "thanks" is said, the One being thanked will hear gibberish and refuse to acknowledge the gesture. I really do think that the One being thanked is appreciative of *every* thankful gesture.

Ezekiel is, of course, famous because it seems that his observation of an unidentified flying object is one of the earliest to have been recorded. That, however, should be considered little more than a footnote in the experiences of this prophet of God. He was given a quite awesome and unenviable task. The people of Israel had divided themselves into two separate and distinct nations. It turns out that God wasn't all that pleased with the arrangement and picked Ezekiel to be the one to make this omniscient displeasure known. As we can infer from the words he used to say it, he at least tried to make the people see that reunification would be something for which to be thankful.

I'm of the notion that it's time for Ezekiel to start talking again about God's desire that all people be one people. We're wasting our time otherwise.

A Most Taxing Call

He saw Levi son of Alphaeus sitting at the tax booth, and he said to him
"Follow me." And he got up and followed him. (Mark 2:14)

My form 1040 accompanied by 243 different schedules covering everything from my itemized deductions to my investments in oil rigs off the coast of Madagascar arrived today (January 2). The folks at the Internal Revenue Service don't waste any time, do they? They want to make sure that the government has received every last bit of our income that the law allows. But then, that's their job … collecting taxes. Unfortunately, they bear the brunt of the tax paying public's ire when, as I said, it's their job. I even have a friend who works for one of the more prominent tax preparation services and she bears her share of that ire. Gosh, all she's doing is helping people wade through the maze of paperwork! It just seems like the people responsible for making sure we pay taxes are at the top of the list of those we love to not love.

Levi was one of those government-employed tax collectors. However, there was a major difference in his case. The government that employed him was not his own government. He lived in a country that was occupied by a larger, stronger government and which was being made to pay taxes to that larger, stronger government even though its seat of power was hundreds of miles away. Levi, realizing that he had to feed the wife and kids, and knowing that he was good with numbers, took the opportunity available to him and went to work collecting those taxes. In so doing he was reviled, even hated by his fellow citizens. They viewed him as a traitor, not only to his country and his people, but to his faith.

Then, Mark says, one day Jesus happened by the office where Levi worked. Without even breaking stride as he passed, Jesus looked Levi in the eye and said, "Let's go." That took a lot of nerve, don't you think? We don't even know if Jesus had ever met Levi. What's even stranger is that, as Mark tells it, Levi didn't even say, "Let me grab my hat," or "Who are you and why do you look so serene?" Mark says simply, "He got up and followed him."

Who among us could do what Levi did? When Jesus walks by and without breaking stride looks at us and says, "Let's go," how do we respond?

I don't like having to figure taxes. I'd rather play the mandolin.

Grandma Burden

On the Sabbath he began to teach in the synagogue, and many who heard him were astounded. They said … "Is not this the carpenter …?" (Mark 6:2-3)

I learned today that Norma Burden died. She was always Grandma Burden to me. Norma was no actual relation of mine, but she was Grandma Burden just the same. If United Methodists made people saints, she would very definitely be Saint Norma by now.

In 1963, my mother was asked to play the piano at the Morris Chapel Methodist Church. I was 11 years old at the time, and she insisted on dragging me along. I don't remember much about the place prior to meeting Grandma Burden. She could see that there were many young folks like me sitting there in those pews with "deer in the headlights" looks in our eyes because 1) we didn't understand what was going on or, 2) we just didn't care about what was going on because it was really boring! So, Grandma Burden decided to do something about it. With the approval of the pastor and the church hierarchy, she started what came to be known as junior church.

After the weekly announcements were done and the first song had been sung, Grandma Burden would stand up, and that was the signal for the young folks to follow her downstairs. Once we got there, Grandma Burden would set up an old easel with a flannel board on it, and start telling us Bible stories using cut-outs that she had made herself. Unlike the pastor who was upstairs warning the people about the dangers of not being "saved," Grandma Burden told us about a God who loved us more than it was possible for us to be loved. Not only that, she made it plain that she also loved us more than it was possible for us to be loved. To paraphrase Mark, she began to teach in the church, and we were astounded!

I have no hesitation in saying that because of the God that Grandma Burden introduced me to, I decided to be baptized and have spent the past 43 years trying from time to time to serve that same God as best I can. She didn't have any fancy education or credentials, nor did she have many years of experience when I knew her. I suppose it would have been easy to question her qualifications. Like

Jesus, she didn't make her living in the service of the church. But she did pour her whole self into telling children about a God they could understand, and she loved every child as though he/she was her own.

God, one of the good ones has come home.

I Believe; Help My Unbelief!

"I believe; help my unbelief!" (Mark 9:24)

If ever there was a more profound statement of faith made in the history of humankind, I'm not aware of it. "I believe; help my unbelief!" These are words uttered in absolute desperation by a father who had watched his son be subjected to seizures for the boy's entire life. In the father's understanding what was happening to his son was the result of a demon. I guess that's a matter of interpretation; for many people epilepsy certainly is a "demon" of sorts. Anyway, the father makes his declaration of faith after having said to Jesus that, if he were able, it surely would be nice if Jesus could fix up his boy, and after Jesus basically responded by saying, "If? If, you say?"

"I believe; help my unbelief!" There is not an honest human being on the face of the earth that would deny that this is *their* statement of faith, as well. Belief in something we can't prove is a pretty tenuous proposition at best. It's easy to say, "I believe." It's another thing to lie in bed in the middle of the night after things haven't gone as we'd hoped and find ourselves saying, "Help my unbelief." The spiritual part of our humanity wants desperately to believe in something or Someone greater than us. It just doesn't make any sense for what we know to be real to be all there is. On the other hand, the human, rational, practical part of our nature always seems to be there somewhere saying, "Yeah, right!"

Every once in a while the spiritual reality impinges upon the human, rational, practical reality in such a way as to leave us with only one possible proclamation: "I believe; help my unbelief." The father who uttered this phrase was on the verge of one of those experiences. I had one of those experiences on the side of a mountain in the Ozarks a few years ago. It was quite disconcerting.

FINAL THOUGHT

Who's Right; Who's Wrong; Who Cares?

"Whoever is not against us is for us." (Mark 9:40)

Here we have a pretty innocent little seven word sentence. It doesn't seem too remarkable until you consider who said it. The disciples were whining because they found out that somebody down the road was casting out a few demons and mentioning Jesus when they did so. The disciples were so upset about it that they tried to get the person to stop. Why? "…. because he was not following us." They figured there was only one way to get it done and it was their way.

Does that sound familiar? There are something like four hundred fifty two trillion groups all claiming to be "Christian." Why is this so? This is so because somebody wasn't following somebody else. Somebody decided that they didn't have to do things like somebody else. Somebody decided that somebody was singing the wrong songs, or reading the wrong Bible, or ordaining people of the wrong gender. In other words, people have continued to act just like those disciples did. They get all upset if everybody isn't following them, to use the disciples' words. What's worse is when the name of Jesus is invoked by people who aren't following them. It never ceases to amaze me that the most doctrinally intolerant people in the world are those who claim to be followers of a man who preached and lived tolerance and insisted that it was the appropriate lifestyle. I just don't get that at all. That's why I'm faithful … but I'm not religious.

Jesus responded to the disciples that day, and he responds to every would-be disciple who has come along since then with one pretty innocent little seven word sentence. "Whoever is not against us is for us."

Get over yourselves already, Christians. Life is too short!

References

2006 Daily Bible Reading Guide. (n.d.). Retrieved December 30, 2005 from
http://www.bibleresourcecenter.org/index/dailybiblereading.dsp

Kee, H. (Ed.). (1989). *The Cambridge Annotated Study Bible:New Revised Standard Version.* New York, NY: Cambridge University Press.

978-0-595-40581-
0-595-40581-9

Printed in the United States
79375LV00003B/151-180

9 780595 405817